This Too Shall Pass

by
Candace Joyner

Copyright © 2020 Candace Joyner
All rights reserved.
ISBN: 978-0-578-61080-1

Published, produced & written by Candace Joyner Publishing
Lumberton, NC 28358

This book or parts thereof may not be reproduced in any form, stored in retrieval system, or transmitted in any form by any means—electronic, mechanical, photocopy, recording, or otherwise—without written permission of the publisher.

Unless otherwise noted, all Scripture quotations are taken from King James Version®. Copyright© 2020. All rights reserved.

Scriptures quotations marked NIV are taken from the Holy Bible, New International Version®, NIV®, Copyright 1973, 1978, 1984, 2011, by Biblica, Inc. ® Used by permission. All rights reserved.

Scriptures quotations marked the New King James Version®. Copyright © 1982 by Thomas Nelson. Used by permission. All right reserved. Printed in the USA

DEDICATION

This book is dedicated to my amazingly beautiful daughters, Justace Rashuan and Jordin McKenzie. It is with profound honor I have reached this milestone and historic moment for our lives. I dedicate this masterpiece to you. Mommy loves you, and this kind of love is beyond measure.

ACKNOWLEDGMENTS FROM PARENTS

I am very proud of you and what you have accomplished in your life. Always know that I love you and will continue to do what is possible to help you along the way.

Your Mother, Mary

I love you, sweetie. You did it again! Your father is so proud of you. I always knew there was something special about you, daughter. The things you have accomplished, I am not surprised. Keep enjoying whatever makes you happy,

Your Father, Dennis.

Contents

Chapter One
    Where It All Started 1

Chapter Two
    God, Is This Real? 10

Chapter Three
    By Prayer And Fasting 18

Chapter Four
    Happy Birthday, Justace 21

Chapter Five
    When God Speaks, Obey 24

Chapter Six
    Not Taking "No" For An Answer 29

Chapter Seven
    God Said Let There Be Light, Day One 35

Chapter Eight
    Thankful Persistence 40

Chapter Nine
    Foundations 45

Chapter Ten
    You Made A Way 56

Chapter Eleven
    Let Us Make Man In Our Image 61

Chapter Twelve
    Don't Stay Stuck 63

Chapter Thirteen
    The Long Walk 70

Chapter Fourteen
    Scriptures To Empower You To Trust God 83

Chapter One
Where It All Started

In 2004, I became pregnant. I already knew that our daughter's name would be Justace. Justace's name is a combination of both parents' names; the first four letters of her father's name (J-U-S-T) and the last three letters of my name (A-C-E). This pregnancy was both exciting and scary for me. I was married to a military serviceman and living in Norfolk, Virginia. We had been married for almost two years. It was a little scary because our lease would soon expire, and he was getting out of the military. Resources were dwindling, and soon after, we were homeless, living in and out of hotels, and sneaking in and out of the military base, staying in the barracks. From time to time, we would spend the night with other military families that we had come to know during our stay in Norfolk. I was excited to be giving birth. However, I was reminded of my previous pregnancy and wondered if I had any cause for concern this time around.

In 2002, as a 19-year-old college freshman in the fall semester, I experienced a molar pregnancy, an abnormal form of pregnancy in which a non-viable fertilized egg implants in the uterus and will fail to come to term. A molar pregnancy can develop when a fertilized egg does not contain an original maternal nucleus. This pregnancy was difficult for me. I was afraid to return home, and I wanted to finish the semester at least. On the contrary, my body said, "NO!" Reluctantly, I returned home, and my family saw how sick I was. They took me to the doctor. I couldn't keep any food down, and I was always tired. I remember saying "God, I feel like I am dying." At the time, I was "2-3" months along. When the technician conducted my first ultrasound, they immediately knew something was wrong. However, according to protocol, I had to wait for the doctor to inform me. I didn't know what exactly was wrong, but one thing I did know was that I felt horrible and if this is how pregnancy felt, I was never getting pregnant again. Finally, the doctor viewed the ultrasound and contacted me to come in for an appointment. Dr. Cummings informed me that this type of pregnancy usually occurs once in every "one thousand pregnancies" but generally in other countries.

He said, "Candace, I have some good news, and I have bad news." I was already feeling like a failure, and I was ashamed that the smart young woman that made all A's in her senior year of high school was now leaving her first year of college due to an unplanned pregnancy. So, Dr. Cummings said, "I'm going to inform you of the bad news first. - this molar pregnancy could kill you."

I looked at him and thought to myself, "This can kill me, I'm only 19, and I haven't had a chance to live out my dreams. I always wanted to finish college, get married, have children, travel the world, and accomplish so many things." It was as if my entire world caved in on me. I held back my tears as much as I could until they endlessly ran down my face.

He continued, "The positive news is that we can perform surgery, and if everything goes well, you will live and you can have more children." His next statement commanded my attention: "If you have pastors, I suggest you go and let them pray with you."

I thought, "Wow... my pastors- I have to face them, oh God!"

Growing up in my home, the church provided a foundation in my life that has taught me much of what I comprehend spiritually. It gave me a hunger to seek God, His word and honor it. From my youth to adulthood, I have watched these pastors lead God's people. So, when the doctor suggested that I call my pastors for prayer, I did. I knew that I didn't want to leave the world just yet. I also had a strong desire to get through all of this and live out my dreams.

I remember barely getting through the weekend. I felt like I was going to die. I will never forget the changes my body went through and the feelings I felt. In a matter of two days, I dropped fifteen pounds; I remember going to the bathroom to take a shower, and sliding down the wall because I didn't have any strength. I finally made it to the shower, and I prayed, "God, I don't want to die. God, I don't want to die right now, I'm too young to die. God, I need much more time than this, please forgive me and please let me live. GOD, DON'T LET ME DIE!"

I want to encourage someone who is facing a storm, and it appears you have hit a dead end. Don't quit and don't give up on your dreams. Sometimes, our choices make us think it's too late and everyone will criticize us for what we've done. I'm here to inform you: No, it's not too late! At this point, what you need to do is get your reward out of it. Don't go through the pain of it and lose your benefits. I don't care what you did and how bad it was; it is not the end of the world. Some things may require you asking for forgiveness, apologizing, releasing past hurts, just to make things right. Do whatever is necessary to get the reward! Let your response and actions include The Word. Let it be graced with love. Do unto others as you would want them to do unto you.

I remember the surgery (D &C) was scheduled early one morning. During such a tender part of my early adulthood, I was so emotional and scared. This procedure was one that most women with complicated pregnancies have in later years, at a time when they are mature enough to handle it. I come from a praying family, and I remember my family praying for me. Oh, how I thank God for a grandmother, a mother, uncles, and aunties that prayed for me without ceasing. I don't know where I would be without prayer. The beautiful thing is I don't even have to wonder about it because I am here because someone prayed.

I want to ask you a question: how often do you take time out to pray for a family member, a loved one, or a friend? Now, I'm going to ask a more intense question: how often do you pray for someone that has wronged you, an enemy or someone that hurt you? I have learned over the years that praying for those who you love and care about isn't enough. I gained so much strength regarding how to deal with and handle the people that have hurt me and walked away from me. It seems the more I prayed, the better I felt. When I encountered those individuals, I felt the peace and assurance that God has heard my prayers. I just merely prayed for them, even when I didn't know specific details of what to pray for. I would urgently and fervently call their names out to God in prayer. Yes, I call their name out, because it's not always easy to pray for them, but that is a start to seek help from God concerning how to go about the situation. Of course, we are to forgive them. The word of God proclaims this method to us in The King James version:

Mark 11:25

"And when ye stand praying, forgive, if ye have ought against any: that your Father also which is in heaven may forgive you your trespasses."

Matthew 6:14

"For if ye forgive men their trespasses, your heavenly Father will also forgive you:"

Luke 6:37

"Do not judge, and you will not be judged. Do not condemn, and you will not be condemned. Forgive, and you will be forgiven."

Ephesians 4:32

"And be ye kind one to another, tenderhearted, forgiving one another, even as God for Christ's sake hath forgiven you."

Colossians 3:13

"Forbearing one another, and forgiving one another, if any man have a quarrel against any: even as Christ forgave you, so also do ye."

I enjoy that the Word of God serves as an operator's manual. It provides clear direction and instructions that apply to our situations. So often, our flesh leads us to believe that holding on to past hurt and circumstances is the best thing to do. We harm ourselves when we choose to hold onto hurt and unusual circumstances that we didn't deserve. Holding onto these things diminishes our strength, joy, and peace. Those losses are detrimental because we need our strength, joy, and peace to be full so that we make it on a day-to-day basis.

It's amazing how I'm discussing the molar pregnancy and how the Holy Spirit has used it as an avenue for me to share a topic about prayers and praying for others. It is rewarding to know that God trusts us to intercede on behalf of sometimes, challenging persons. However, prayer is the key that unlocks the door to peace of mind. When you walk in the spirit of prayer in this manner, what the person did or did not do to you will no longer be a concern. In prayer, you find avenues of strength that motivate you to obey the word concerning the situation. Prayer shifts your focus from the issue and places it in the hands of God. Watch this, it would be difficult to pray in faith about a situation and God will not prick your heart about what you should do and you do not obey. Prayer is an opportunity to give it to God, and in return, He gives you what you need. Usually, it is instructions or a reminder of what the word of God already instructs us to do. We must become obedient to what God says, so we can win. Remember the victory already belongs to us. Some may say, "Well I don't hear God speaking to me." The truth is that God is always speaking, the question is, "are we listening". When you pray, you should make a practice of sitting in a quiet place so you can hear God. You also can begin by writing in a journal after you pray. Yes, write what's on your mind and what's in your heart immediately after you pray. Through writing after prayer, hearing activation begins. What's in you will become exposed. I believe your obedience in this area will bring clarity to you about your life. In addition to clarity, obedience will cause you to eat the fruit thereof!

Isaiah 1: 19 "If ye be willing and obedient, ye shall eat the good of the land." 20 "But if ye refuse and rebel, ye shall be devoured with the sword: for the mouth of the LORD hath spoken it."

I went in for surgery that morning. The procedure was called a dilation and curettage (D&C.) It was removing what was growing in my abdomen. In the molar pregnancy, the baby wasn't developing normally. Something was growing, but it wasn't in the form of a baby. There was no heartbeat and only clumps of growing tissue.

I understand that many of you would have probably never heard of such a thing. I know I never did until the doctors informed me. Therefore, you can imagine what was going through my mind at the age of 19 when I heard this information. I bless God that I made it out alive. I remember when I woke up after the surgery, the technicians were hovering over me, calling my name. "Candace, Candace, Candace, wake up, it's all over." I remember thinking, "Oh my, I'm alive!" I honestly didn't know what was going to happen. I just know that when I heard my name, I had another chance.

God, I thank you for taking me through that difficult time and allowing me to live. The pain of the reality of losing a child hurt, but I found healing and solace through my faith in God. My faith in God increased at the age of 19 because I remember praying to God asking Him to allow me to live despite the doctor's words, "this can kill you!" Some things in your life were meant to kill you but didn't. Anytime you outlive something, it is because there's a purpose for your life! Why not give birth to your purpose? You made it out. You outlived the very thing that tried to kill you. You're so much stronger, and because of it, you're a better person. God had answered me, and for that, I am thankful and humbly appreciative.

I began to walk in adulthood after this experience. I got married in less than a year. I had a very challenging marriage. There were both excellent and pivotal moments. I wrapped myself in a lot of pain because I believed what happened at home stayed at home. Let me pause for a moment and make this disclaimer, "What goes on in my house stays in my house" is a lie from the pits of hell if things are not healthy. Embracing this type of thinking can potentially destroy you depending on the situation. Some things have happened and are probably still happening right now, and some of you need to cry out loud and talk to somebody. I charge you to call the police, call a professional to help you if you are in need. Now, I'm not implying that you should tell your business and discuss personal relationship matters with everyone. Not by any means at all. Don't share with your family, friends, and loved ones about your marriage and personal matters. When I say talk to someone, I mean someone who offers professional insight and resources if you are living in unhealthy or unfavorable conditions which include but not limited to abuse and adultery.

There was a time when I didn't even have toilet tissue in my home. Here I am, suffering and didn't have the very necessity of toilet paper. I remember going through this time of abandonment and praying to God for a change. In my mind, I was so young and dumb and didn't know how to reach out for help in so many areas. I was left alone living in another state. I just cried myself through it. I didn't know I was supposed to get help and tell somebody. Because as a young girl, I was told, "What happens in your house, stays in your house." I thought, "This will soon pass and better days are coming." I remember when it got so bad, and I thought "you better get yourself a job." I landed a job at Victoria's Secret. But without a car, I was forced to walk to the nearest bus stop, only to walk through a territory that belonged to three prostitutes. So, what did they do? Yeah, they thought they could push on me and confront me. I remember being afraid and thinking, "Lord, I'm just trying to pay my bills and buy myself some tissue and necessities that I need in life." So now, I'm 19, living in a big city with all this warfare going on. I remember getting on the bus, and man, I saw people from all walks of life. The bus can be a scary ride for someone from the country. I was scared, but I rode it in the hopes of getting through this difficult time. I was thinking, "Lord, how am I going to pay all these bills?"

One day, the strangest thing happened to me while I was working at Victoria Secret. The atmosphere of this store was very romantic; many couples shopped there. Due to my current situation, my marriage was primarily on the rocks at this point; when my spouse was there, the warfare in our home was intense and very stressful. One day, I observed this couple walking hand in hand, and they started kissing. That moment struck me with a vengeance. Tears just ran down my face. I was thinking, "How can my marriage be so bad, we were so in love at one time." Not knowing how to answer that question, the tears just continued to flow, and I cried uncontrollably till the moment I went to the break room.

I talked to my supervisor and informed her that I was having marital problems, didn't know where my spouse was, and I couldn't function at work. I just remember being in so much pain and I couldn't take it anymore. Readers, please understand I was also unlearned in so many ways; I was only 19. I was just in a place of pain. This type of emotional pain turned into physical pain, and it was unbearable at times. I didn't know this type of pain could manifest into sleepless nights, headaches and back pain. I remember later in life, realizing that this wasn't just my pain. I began to understand as I became spiritually mature, that what I was going through would possibly help both men and women. Now 15 years later, I receive countless testimonies. I knew I could tell my testimony and help people experience deliverance. Not to talk about it and belittle anyone, but share my testimony at the appropriate time. Sharing your testimony versus gossip/venting/bashing someone is different.

It was later during the year 2007 or 2008 that I went through it again, and I was hurting. I heard a soft voice, "This is not just your pain you feel, but it's some of who you will help throughout your life." I remember thinking, I don't want this. Have you ever hurt so bad because of a traumatic experience and the emotional pain turned physical? My body would literally ache. When the emotional pain transforms into physical pain, you are at a very intense period of your life, you need God, and you need people to assist you. You need help. I repeat you need help.

Going back to the age of 19, when I was just hurting, I knew the one thing I could do, and this is the key theme throughout this book: PRAY! I also remember during that time, I started lying in my bed for hours and hours in the morning, and I felt as if I didn't have a life. I remember thinking, "What's the use?" But my spirit would say, "God is the use." And "What's the point, Candace?" My spirit would decree, "God is the point!" NO matter what's happening, know this that this too shall pass! Yes, I would pray. But what prayer did was give me the wisdom to get out and to get help. Don't have a prayer life and not obey God-Prayer ushers you to obedience and into God's will. Prayer rescues you!

Chapter Two
God, Is This Real?

Another trying time before I became pregnant with Justace was infidelity in my marriage. I remember hearing the female on the other line, and that almost destroyed me. I felt like I already knew there was someone else, but this conversation provided me with the evidence. This crushed me because it was as if I was reliving what I saw as a child growing up. I always said I would have a beautiful marriage. Don't we all? My parents also went through similar things that I faced in my marriage. It was as if I'm reliving what I saw my parents go through. I remember going through that moment when I realized that I am re-living exactly what my parents went through. How does this happen? I mean especially after being in love. I've spoken a great deal concerning challenging times, but we were very much in love in the beginning. This was a love that no one could question. We were young, but we intended to love each other until the end, have children and live the American dream.

Nevertheless, the infidelity was destroying me as well, dealing with a spouse who was already contemplating suicide, abandoning me, and going through childhood issues in his adult life. All these things began to take a toll on me. Because he or I never received the proper counseling for his childhood tragedies, our marriage had only intensified them. Marriage never makes your life better; it magnifies what's already there. We both dragged childhood trauma into our loving marriage which eventually began to eat it up and led to destruction. Life was just hard for this 19-year-old girl. I remember after finding out about this woman, I began to suffer from depression and low self-esteem. I blamed myself and became very insecure. My first thought was nobody else would ever want me. I was so confused in my mind and needed to reach out to someone. So, I reach out to God. I couldn't face myself in the mirror because I was crazy enough to convince myself that I was not attractive and she must look better than I do. As I said, I was 19, and I didn't understand any of this. When I walked into the bathroom and saw myself in the mirror, I would cry. I felt like a failure and that I would never get past my current situation.

That's how it is when you're in a storm, you feel like you are never coming out of it. The storm is all you can see and feel. Every day was getting worse. That's what led to the long hours lying in bed. I would lie there as if nothing was going to get better. During this time, I met a beautiful lady that ministered to me. She prophesied to me about writing a book one day and telling my story. I remember looking at the phone like, "who is this person". Well, one day I got enough courage to get up. I felt as if I was losing my mind. I felt my mind leaving me and drifting away like the waves of the sea. I felt like I had no purpose to live. Soon after experiencing this, the greater one on the inside picked me up.

1 John 4:4 "because greater is he that is in you, than he that is in the world."

Ezekiel 36:27 "And I will put my spirit within you, and cause you to walk in my statutes."

In my mind, I thought, "Candace, when all fails, pray." I remember growing up in a ministry that was full of prayer. Oh my, there are page length prayers that many of us know by heart because we prayed them so much. My God, we would get to church super early, pray for one full hour. Sometimes prayers will overflow into regular service causing it to start late. I also remember as a little girl, going to shut-ins and praying as long as I could. I also remember my mother, teaching my sister and myself how to pray. My God, she would make us lay prostrate and say, "Candace and Dee, y'all need to pray." I want to tell you; I was becoming so tired of praying. But today, I am glad that those prayers are still paying off. I almost forgot we had the 24-hour prayer time a few days a week. Each family had an hour to pray.

Some days, however, the Holy Spirit would lead the pastors and us; we would have prayers every single day at church. Prayer is in my roots-I know prayer. It is a vital part of my spiritual upbringing. I'm glad I grew up in the house of the Lord. I'm talking about attending church every Sunday, Bible study, conference, and revival. My mother kept us in the house of the Lord. It is imperative, especially for the day and times we're living in today. We must stay within the church. More so, we should make sure the church is in us. Now, there are cases where church hurt occurs, and the church does not exemplify Christ as it should. But that's not a reason for us to stop or give up entirely on the church. Assemble yourself in the house of God consistently by having a church home. The following passages of scripture are powerful and speak to us about the gathering of the saints together.

Psalm 133:1 "Behold, how good and how pleasant it is for brethren to dwell together in unity!" 2 "It is like the precious ointment upon the head, that ran down upon the beard, even Aaron's beard: that went down to the skirts of his garments;" 3 "As the dew of Hermon, and as the dew that descended upon the mountains of Zion: for there the LORD commanded the blessing, even life for evermore."

Hebrews 10:25 "Not forsaking the assembling of ourselves together, as the manner of some is; but exhorting one another: and so much the more, as ye see the day approaching."

My roots are in the church; it's my connection to how I became spiritually in tune with God. The intense praying I learned caused the power of praying and interceding to be very relevant in my life. I was in a very broken time in my life, yet my mind ushered me to believe in prayer. I was encouraged to pray.

Amid all the chaos, hurt, pain, and shame, can you still pray? Now life will get hard and life will throw you a bad hand but will your mind still lead you to pray? Will you pray when all hell breaks loose? Will you pray when you don't feel like it? Will you pray when someone walks out on you? Will you pray when it seems all hope is gone? Will you still pray when everything is going well? When you can remain faithful in prayer regardless of your storm, it shows you where your faith is.

My mind drove me to prayer. Either I was going to pray, or I was going to lose it. Either I was going to pray, or I was going to die! Let me explain, death is not always physical, it can be spiritual, mental, social, financial, and so on and so forth! Honestly, if I ever become spiritually dead, then I am dead. Listen, the Bible says according to Zechariah 4: 6, "Not by might, nor by power, but by my spirit." Much of what we face today is a spiritual matter. We are living in human bodies; we are spiritual beings. Let me provide scriptural revelation:

John 14: "Even the Spirit of truth; whom the world cannot receive, because it seeth him not, neither knoweth him: but ye know him; for he dwelleth with you, and shall be in you."

1 Corinthians 2:14 "But the natural man receiveth not the things of the Spirit of God: for they are foolishness unto him: neither can he know them, because they are spiritually discerned."

Romans 8:9 "But ye are not in the flesh, but in the Spirit, if so be that the Spirit of God dwells in you. Now if any man have not the Spirit of Christ, he is none of his."

Romans 8:11 "But if the Spirit of him that raised up Jesus from the dead dwell in you, he that raised up Christ from the dead shall also quicken your mortal bodies by his Spirit that dwelleth in you."

1 Corinthians 3:16 "Know ye not that ye are the temple of God, and that the Spirit of God dwelleth in you."

I got up the nerve to get out of bed one day and as my mind began to recollect on my spiritual upbringing. I got my Bible, and I remember doing something that felt a little awkward. I held my Bible up high as I could, and I said, "GOD, IS THIS REAL"? "God, if all this stuff is really REAL, I want to know it and understand it in a very profitable way" I will never forget that moment. I was at my breaking point. There was so much going on in the life of this 19-year-old girl who was ready for God to change her life. I found out I wanted God for myself and nobody else.

After I held my Bible up, immediately, I knew that I had to bring my mind under subjection. Subjection to what you may ask? To anything other than giving up. In order to step out of the depression, I had to focus my mind on God, anything contrary to living had to go. My mind was only subject to anything that was going to bring me out. The first thing I did was to write out decrees and hung them on every wall in my home. It was just me anyway; I didn't have much company, and at that point, if anybody came, I didn't care about what they thought. I was reclaiming both my life back and peace of mind. When you become desperate for what you are entitled to, there's nothing no one can do to stop, block, or hinder your breakthrough. When you want it bad enough, it's yours. We can very well look at the woman with the issue of blood. She had dealt with this sickness for twelve long years. What was the difference between the first year or the fifth or maybe even the tenth year? It wasn't until the twelfth year when she made the best decision that caused her to be healed. That's what we must do, make decisions that will cause us to be healed and to live.

Why do we wait so long to decide whether or not we're going to keep wasting time? Wasn't this breakthrough long overdue for her? I mean one year was enough for me. But this woman was sick for twelve long years. It wasn't until that twelfth year, until she said, "If I can but touch the hem of His garment, I will be made whole." The passage reads:

Mark 5: 25 "And a certain woman, which had an issue of blood twelve years," 26 "And had suffered many things of many physicians, and had spent all that she had, and was nothing bettered, but rather grew worse," 27 "When she had heard of Jesus, came in the press behind, and touched his garment." 28 "For she said If I may touch but his clothes, I shall be whole." 29 "And straightway the fountain of her blood was dried up; she felt in her body that she was healed of that plague." 30 "And Jesus, immediately knowing in himself that virtue had gone out of him, turned him about in the press, and said, Who touched my clothes?" 31 "And his disciples said unto him, Thou seest the multitude thronging thee, and sayest thou, Who touched me?" 32 "And he looked round about to see her that had done this thing." 33 "But the woman fearing and trembling, knowing what was done in her, came and fell down before him, and told him all the truth." 34 "And he said unto her, Daughter, thy faith hath made thee whole; go in peace and be whole of thy plague."

I said to myself God, what was different about the woman with the issue of blood touching him and all the people already surrounding Him. Why did He recognize the woman that touched Him? I began to dig a little deeper, and I studied the original Greek meaning of this word touch. It wasn't an ordinary touch. The Greek word for touch here is *hepatmai*- it means "TO ATTACH ONESELF", and it means "RELATIONS". This touch wasn't ordinary. To who or what are you attached? With who or what are you to in a relationship? Let's dissect this a little further. The word "ATTACH" means to fasten, affix or to connect. It also means to join in action or function. Let's also observe the term relations. "RELATIONS" means a principle whereby the effect is given to an act done at one time as if it had been done at a previous time. This word relations also means a logical or natural association between two or more things.

It was a natural association between two or more things. This woman knew by nature she was associated with Jesus and reaching out to Him was her final option or death would be her destination. I can imagine her saying, "I might as well reach out and touch Him, what do I have to lose?" Could it be we are reaching out and attaching ourselves to the wrong things and people? Is this why we're not progressing forward into wholeness? Then Jesus sealed it and told her to go in peace and be whole of thy plague. In other words, what was stopping her wasn't any longer; her faith produced wholeness in her life.

This interpretation of this intimate encounter says a mouth full. We see clearly that this woman attached herself to Jesus. This touch also signifies her desire for a relationship with Jesus. In other words, she considered, I had relations with the doctors, yet I have lost it all, so now, I'm attaching my life to yours. Sometimes, it's not until we spent it all, and when there's no one else around to confide in that we can attach ourselves and build relations with the Almighty God. I was likened to the woman with the issue. I didn't necessarily have an issue of blood, but I did have a plethora of issues, and I was desperate. As the woman pressed her way through the crowds, I pressed my way through all the problems I was facing in my own life. I said, "Whatever I got to do to get to you, I'm going to do it, and I did. I first put a sign in my bedroom. I know Holy Spirit inspired this sign because it read, "Candace, do not lay in bed today. Candace, GET UP. CANDACE IF YOU ARE READING THIS SIGN, IT MEANS YOU WOKE UP TODAY, AND ITS IMPERATIVE THAT YOU GET OUT OF BED. GET UP AND PRAY!" Yes, I had to be obedient and first, tell myself that my situation was not going to allow me to have an excuse and stay depressed. I needed to inform myself, "Ma'am, you're not wasting your life in this bed, there is plenty to do. Not to mention just a year ago, God spared your life when you endured the molar pregnancy." So I learned how to get out of bed every morning by reading that sign. And I want you to know that having that sign posted in my house helped me out so much. I got up and would proceed downstairs. I had written signs all over my home and hung them up on the walls. From the bedroom, bathroom, hallway, stairway, living area, kitchen, and laundry room, affirmations covered the walls. I needed reminders all around me not to quit. I wrote out Bible verses and positive declarations on each of these signs for me to progress and make it during that time. Readers, I had to see it before I could believe it. I had to get it in my mind that I wasn't going to die early. I was desperate. My spirit was rejoicing knowing that this too shall pass!

Chapter Three
By Prayer And Fasting

I knew that if I was going to make it, I needed to pray. I also incorporated fasting, and I began to read the word of God like never before. That Bible I held up before God became my help, aid, and guide. I read the word for hours at the time. I prayed fervently and endlessly like it was an 8 -5, I mean sometimes longer than that. I was too weak at the time to work, so I end up quitting the job at Victoria Secrets. I was too stressed to wait on customers and adhere to the policies and procedures.

Furthermore, I didn't have a vehicle and riding the city bus wasn't safe for me. It took about two to three weeks before making up mind to do something different. So now, I'm fasting as well. I began to pray early in the morning till sundown, lying before God. I remember the time going by and it didn't faze me at all. I knew I needed something significant from God. I wanted life, my peace back, and I wanted my marriage. I wanted my husband home. Therefore, I prayed, and I waited. I fasted, and I waited. I read the Bible, and I waited. I wasn't as hurt as I was before. I wasn't as weak as I was weeks before. The fantastic thing about this was I was 19 years old. I say the power of God moved on my behalf again. The first day after the fast, my husband (at the time) walked through the door. I remember thinking, "Wow God, does it work like that?" And I'm here to tell you that the word, prayer, and fasting does work! I am a living witness!!!

Matthew 17:20 "Because of your unbelief: for verily I say unto you, If you have faith as a grain of mustard seed, you shall say unto this mountain, Remove from here to yonder place; and it shall remove, and nothing shall be impossible unto you." 21 "But this kind goes not out but by prayer and fasting."

Things began to change remarkably in my life, and I bless God for it. Did the trials stop? No, they didn't, but my faith had increased, and my strength came back. I also began to experience peace. Now, it's one thing to experience a storm without any peace and almost lose your mind. But it's another story to experience pain and go through the worst storms of life and still have peace. The difference is you're able to manage and get through it. You're able to rest and do what's necessary for your life and not break or settle for what the enemy is bringing your way. I thank God for sending peace. I want to leave with you these scriptures before I enter the next chapter.

1 Thessalonians 5:23 "And the very God of peace sanctify you wholly."

Philippians 4:7 "And the peace of God, which passeth all understanding, shall keep your hearts and minds through Christ Jesus."

Psalm 107:20 "He sent his word, and healed them, and delivered them from their destructions."

As I stated, my husband returned home and I became pregnant with our first girl. I had her name already figured out. I said her name is going to be Justace. The challenge at hand was that only after a few months being pregnant, our only means of income was coming to an end. Justace's father was getting put out of the military. Our lease was up, and we were without a place to live. Homeless and pregnant. I remember sneaking into the barracks with my husband at that time. He, of course, got in trouble when someone saw me and reported me. I wasn't supposed to be staying there. Then we found out about a cheap hotel on base and lodged there. Other times, we spent the night at friends' houses. I met this saved young preacher who would one day become Justace's Godmother, Stacey! Wow, she was my angel wrapped in flesh. She had other roommates, but she knew we needed a place to lay down.

The pregnancy was very stressful, and I remember I was spotting and needed to go to the hospital. I was told to take it easy, and the spotting finally stopped. Finally, the military discharged my husband, and we moved back to North Carolina with family until we got a new lease. It's now 2005, and I'm almost 20 years old. We were in Durham because I was too ashamed to come back home. My hometown is Lumberton, and honestly, I wanted to finish school where I initially began my college journey, which was North Carolina Central University. We got there, and within a few months, things started to crumble. They crumbled so hard that I had no other choice but to leave Durham and go home as God had previously instructed me to do. Now I'm back and separated again. I was ashamed, and I just wanted my pregnancy to be over. I was ready for my baby to come. My weight jumped from 117 to 197 pounds. I came home, and no one recognized me. My entire body transformed. I realized that I hadn't seen a doctor in about two weeks. I knew that I had to be seen because I was in my last trimester, so off to the doctor I went.

Chapter Four
Happy Birthday, Justace

Happy Birthday Justace July 26, 2005

One day, I was charged to visit the doctor because I was already eight months pregnant with Justace and recently moved backed home. I had transferred my medical records from Durham, but they hadn't called me with an appointment yet. They mentioned it would be in a few days. Well, two weeks had gone by and no phone call. For some reason, well, let me say it correctly, the Holy Spirit had beckoned me to go to the doctor. What was so peculiar about this is, I didn't feel sick; I just knew I needed to see a doctor. At this term in pregnancy, women are to visit the doctor every week, not to mention; I was already high risk. So, I went to the doctor, and again, they told me they would call me because they were busy. I responded and said, "I'm not leaving today, I haven't been seen in two weeks, and I want to see the doctor today." Thank God for my persistence because they allowed me to wait. There wasn't a doctor available, but there was a midwife available to see. Those that know me, know that when I need to change my tone and make something happen, I will. I didn't disrespect anyone; I just felt I needed to see someone that day. Let me explain why I know this was God ordering my steps on July 26, 2005.

So, the midwife checked my vitals and asked, "Mom, how are you feeling?" I said, "Fine." Then I heard, "You will deliver Justace today; your blood pressure is way too high. Do you not feel dizzy or anything?" "No," I responded. They told me to go to Southeastern Regional Medical Center immediately. With me being immature and not understanding the intensity of the situation, my husband and I went to Walmart. I went there to the portrait studio because I realized I hadn't taken professional pictures of the pregnancy and so, I needed to do that. I also ate M&M's because I was hungry and they asked me not to eat. I didn't understand that high blood pressure is a silent killer.

When I finally arrived at the hospital, of course, they wondered what took so long and asked questions. Nevertheless, once again, they took my vitals. That's when the doctors rushed in and said, "We need to go in emergency surgery, and we need to do it now. She blurted out, "Turn off the TV, unplug the phone, and get the family out." They were suggesting the magnitude of the situation and the chances of things taking the wrong turn, and it was important for me to relax my body as much as possible! I was only 21 at the time, and I was afraid. It seemed as much as I wanted to relax, I couldn't. At this point, I knew this was serious. I was thinking, "Why did I go to Wal-Mart to take pictures and why in the world did I eat those M&M's?" Then the doctor said unto me," Candace, may I pray with you before we go into surgery." As a young lady, I thought, "Oh God, this is really serious right now; please let my baby be okay." Immediately, I told her "yes." For a little girl who had grown up in ministry and understood the importance of prayer, I knew when the doctor asked to do it; I realized the seriousness of my current situation. We all needed God and needed Him right then. I needed Him, her father needed Him, Justace needed Him, and the doctor needed Him as she performed the surgery. But what is so amazing is how He ordered my steps that day and took me to the physician's office. Then He demanded that I ask to be seen by the doctors even when they tried to send me back home. Remember this was without me having any symptoms; I felt okay! Now He had provided a Christian doctor to be in the position to deliver Justace and not only that, a praying doctor that was willing to be obedient to the guidance of the Holy Spirit. To this day, I thank God for that doctor.

They put me to sleep and sometime later, I woke up to a seven-pound baby girl. I could not hold Justace for about three days. The medication was so strong that I kept dozing in and out. I finally moved from the labor and delivery hall to a regular room. I stayed in the hospital for about seven days. That cesarean section took a toll on my body and that my friend was some intense pain! Oh my!! It did, BUT THAT TOO DID PASS!!

I felt the need to share with you the early stages of how life was before I gave birth to Justace. Because years later when the doctors informed me that she had cancer was not the beginning of disappointment for me. My life as a young lady was very intense and sometimes unbearable. As a child, I saw things that I will never forget from my upbringing, household, family, church, friends, and life itself. It was at the age of 19 when I began to see the magnitude of a chaotic sad life that Justace was born into it. Today, I am 32 years young, and everything that I have gone through was for a reason. I just decided that this too shall pass and nothing would stop me!

I'm writing this book to tell you that "don't let life stop you because of what has happened! Begin again and watch God move for you." I'm reminded of Philippians 1:6, "Being confident of this very thing, that he which hath begun a good work in you will perform it until the day of Jesus Christ."

Chapter Five
When God Speaks, Obey

KJV Proverbs 3:6 "In all thy ways acknowledge him, and he shall direct thy paths."

KJV Jeremiah 10:23 "O LORD, I know that the way of man is not in himself: it is not in man that walketh to direct his steps."

KJV Proverbs 20:24 "Man's goings are of the LORD; how can a man then understand his own way?"

I can remember so vividly standing in my kitchen during the early winter of 2016. I was near the microwave when I observed my daughter and I heard the words, "Take Justace to the doctor." My first thought was, "What and why?" After asking Justace if she was feeling okay and hurting anywhere? I left the thought alone. I left it alone because she said she felt fine and to me, she looked terrific. She was a unique ten-year-old little girl running around doing the girly stuff that ten-year-olds do. Oh, and not to mention, she's very intrigued with her education. She was embracing that girliness: lip gloss, painting her nails, dressing up, making jewelry, and everything that came with it.

A week later, the thought crossed my mind again and then, I heard, "Take Justace to the doctor." I mentioned it to my mom, and I remember telling my mom that I was going to take Justace to the doctor before I started the spring semester of my final undergraduate degree in Social Work at Fayetteville State University. And I did just that; I took her to the doctor. As they examined her, Justace told the doctor that she hadn't been able to use the bathroom like she used to. They prescribed her a laxative, and we went home. Now with my eyes opened wide, I'm monitoring her bowel movements carefully. Although she had taken the Mira lax, she still could not release properly. As a concerned parent, I took her back to the doctor. This time, I was told to increase her Mira lax. So, we did. The doctors also recommended an X-ray. The X-ray showed that her bowels were being backed up from front to back.

It came to the point where I was examining my daughter's behavior, and I just felt like something wasn't right. I remember many nights, just standing in the doorway observing my daughter, and I said, "God, what is going on?" I felt like something wasn't right. During this time, I thought maybe she's stressed out about something, and I made her an appointment to talk to a professional counselor. After all, this is what I was going to school for, and I sincerely believe in Licensed Counselors. She was a ten-year-old girl who had witnessed her parents separate and divorce with no explanation. I knew stress played a role in her life. Unanswered questions lingered in her mind.

As a mother, I wasn't aware of how to tell my child, that her Father had walked away from his family and moved away. Unaware of the harm I was causing from not talking about it, I didn't say anything at all. I mean, how does one share such details with a daddy's girl that he's gone and has no plans to return? Instead of being negative, I just kept my mouth closed. Knowing what I know now, the truth is the truth. No matter how bad it is, there is always a way for one to discuss a significant life event with their child without speaking negatively about the person involved. Not to mention, Justace's and I had also separated from a ministry she had been a part of, all of her young life. This young girl had experienced so much at an early age, and no doubt was hurting on the inside.

A few weeks had gone by, and I went back to the pediatric clinic with Justace because her symptoms were getting worse. I knew something wasn't right. During this part of our lives, God had interrupted my sleep, and I was going into my children's bedrooms at night, interceding and praying. There is a difference between the two. When one intercedes, they are intervening on someone's behalf. Intercession is when you become that person and stand in the gap for them. When you pray, it's usually a request made unto God. It doesn't matter if it's for you or someone else. Before then, my prayer time in the middle of the night was sporadic, only when God touched me to do so. You better believe there had to be a reason for me to wake up and pray at 2 or 3 am! But this season, it was almost every night, and I would always say God, what is it? I remember thinking about what is going on? Because the urgency in my spirit to go pray and to intercede was now very intense, and I knew God was up to something.

The moment your prayer life increases for someone else is real intercession.

Romans 15:30 "Now I beseech you, brethren, for the Lord Jesus Christ's sake, and for the love of the Spirit, that ye strive together with me in your prayers to God for me......"

Colossians 4:12 "Epaphras, who is one of you, a servant of Christ, saluteth you, always laboring fervently for you in prayers, that ye may stand perfect and complete in all the will of God."

I want to discuss prayer and intercession a little further because we can never underestimate this time with God. I actually enjoy praying most of the time. Now, there are times I don't feel like it and don't want to engage. There are times I'm tired and just want to sleep and not be bothered. During this season of my life when God was calling me to prayer in the middle of the night, the urgency in my spirit superseded any feeling of wanting to lay in bed or being sleepy. So, I would get up and go to my children's bedroom and pray. I remember laying hands on Justace and Jordin during this time. When I got to Justace, I would lay hands on her stomach and say, "I command you to leave her body in the name of Jesus." I remember praying and speaking to her body endlessly because I knew her bowels needed to move and I knew they needed to move fast. This was my nightlife. I bless God for the urgency to pray because what I was speaking to was far bigger than what I knew it to be! We should never underestimate the power of prayer. Prayer positions us to take our eyes off the situation and place our focus on God and our faith in Him. Because what we are facing is major and very difficult and often looks impossible, it takes our faith in God to keep us in a position not to lose hope. I grew weary of giving my child laxatives. I needed God to move for my baby and me. I was so sincere about my walk with God, and I knew that He would attend to us. We could not allow the storm, sickness, infirmities, or challenges to terminate our belief in God. We are to gain strength in the word of God. The word of God is authentic and powerful. So I prayed, and I interceded. When God led me to intercede, I would speak as if I was Justace herself. If we can ever get unselfish and really pray for others, then, we are going somewhere in God. I've interceded for so many people during my time with the Lord, but this time, it was my child, and I knew she needed prayer more than anybody, for whom I had ever interceded. My God, I remember how God would wake me up and have me intercede for people, and I did it. Just out of obedience. It's something when you are interceding for a loved one especially your child. I just knew that I needed to do this for her. I made declarations and decrees for her, her body, and her life. I spoke on her behalf those nights as if it was an emergency, in which it was. My baby needed this, and I left her room many nights, believing and sensing that through my faith, what we needed God to do was already done. I walked away saying, "Oh, her body will show the results when we wake up." It was now weeks since she had a bowel movement. After I prayed, I believed it! The word of God tells us:

Mark 11: 24 "Therefore I say unto you, What things soever ye desire, when ye pray, believe that ye receive them, and ye shall have them."

This scripture was so fitting for me because I believe God would answer me. I made myself believe it. I received it in my spirit. I knew that one day, my prayer would allow for a natural response. What we do in prayer will penetrate in the spirit and give birth to a physical manifestation. I desired for my baby to be whole in her body and free from sickness, disease, and poisons in her body. Here are a few other scriptures to go along with this intense and needed season of prayer:

1 John 3:22 "And whatsoever we ask, we receive of him, because we keep his commandments, and do those things that are pleasing in his sight."

1 John 5:14 "And this is the confidence that we have in him, that, if we ask anything according to his will, he heareth us."

I charge you, whatever it is that you are in need of, whether it's you or someone else, don't stop praying! When you are praying or interceding on someone else's behalf, believe it, receive it, and you shall have it! It will be worth your while and those around you! Understand you are a world shaker and if God allows you to see someone in a situation, pray with them, pray for them, and watch the results come to pass!

Chapter Six
Not Taking "No" For An Answer

I remember not exactly getting the results I wanted and continuously monitoring my daughter and yet seeking for healing in her body. So, I took her back to the doctor, and I remember the doctor saying to me, "Mom, why are you here, you're back again?" I said, "Yes I am!" I explained that she still wasn't able to use the bathroom and I needed someone to see her again, but this time, she needed to be seen by a specialist. The doctor stated that a specialist wasn't needed and having backed up stool could take a while before it's fully released. I already knew that ,because as a concerned mother, I began doing my research concerning my daughter's symptoms. All I could remember was the feeling of something isn't right about this. Only God can provide the instinct to a mother for her child. Holy Spirit dwells within me and that caused me to go back to the doctor because something just wasn't right! It's Jesus himself that tells you in His word: "I have come, that they might have life and that they might have it more abundantly." It states that they "might" I believe this signifies, "How bad do you want life?" You might have it if you do what it takes. I wanted my life back, this was affecting me too. I wanted my daughter to have her life back. I remember thinking if she's not going to the bathroom properly, that stool is just sitting in her and that can't be healthy for her body. It must go now! The doctor said, "Mom, let's increase her Mira lax once again, add stomach massages and leg exercises, and that should get those bowels moving quicker." I said, "Okay!" By this time, my daughter was going to the doctor at least every three weeks. The doctors were feeling her abdomen every time, and each time, they kept saying, "yeah, that poop is still in there, let's give it some time to move." I remember thinking, "This doesn't make sense. I said, "We need to see that specialist; this can't be healthy for her body! "We left like we usually did, but I didn't stop praying. I took the doctor's orders, and I began leg exercises and stomach massages. Although that was not necessarily the right answer, it assured me that I was a woman of God, far from stupid, and yes, full of discernment.

Now, I began running with my daughter consistently, performing leg exercises on her and massaging her stomach. Not to mention the urgency to still pray in the middle of the night because the Holy Spirit had me up, praying and interceding on her behalf. Knowing how I felt in my spirit, I was becoming irritable with what the doctors were telling me because it didn't make sense. Then, I began to compare it to what I believe God was placing in my spirit. Of course, because of my relationship with God, I am spirit-led and must comply with what He's telling me to do. So, after the leg exercises, stomach massages, and increasing laxatives I took my baby back to the doctor. Yes, I did. It was in March, during my spring break, precisely one week before my birthday. I remember telling Justace that I was going to take her out of school because I needed to examine her closer. I also remember taking her off meats and placing her on liquid diets. I can still remember how the lumps felt in her abdomen those long nights when I was praying and laying hands on her. I remember the pain I felt and the intense feelings of 'something isn't right here'. I would cry out unto God and find comfort in Him. I'm so glad that I didn't let go of what I was led to do in my spirit. I remember it like yesterday, Justace and I running around my neighborhood because I said, God if we do this, and comply with doctor's orders, she's going to be okay, and her bowels will move quicker. I would speak positively to her and make our runs fun and interesting until we made it back home. Then after getting home, I would massage her stomach again. I was pressing down on her stomach in hopes that the bowels would loosen up. But one thing I can say, that with all the stomach massages, I mixed it with prayer. I would tell those hard lumps in my daughter's belly, "You got to go, leave her body now! Justace is healed of the Lord; she belongs to God!" I thank God for the power of a praying mother.

I'm so glad that I was in a season where my steps had been ordered to visit this church in Marion SC. It was a church where I found hope and strength. As I stated, we were in ministry transition and that was a place I received some strong spiritual meat. This foundation I received upon entering the hardest time of my life would be well needed for our lives. Bishop teaches that whatever we are doing, do it so God can be glorified. Bring pleasure to Christ's heart and fame to His name!

The final time going to the doctor, I remember waking up and saying "okay, we're going back to the doctor today because I just don't agree with something." I couldn't shake the feeling that something isn't right. It's amazing to have the Holy Spirit because he will lead us and guide us in all truth.

Psalm 25:5 "Lead me in thy truth and teach me: for thou art the God of my salvation; on thee do I wait all day."

Yes, His word is truth to us! In my consistency in seeking Him, He led me to what I needed. "In thee do I wait all the day." Because I couldn't shake the feeling I had, I choose to wait upon the Lord. I knew because I served the Lord with all my heart that it was Him leading me and causing me to discern. I never underestimated my relationship with God. The difference between living for God and serving the enemy is that when I need the correct direction, I can always come to the one that knows all about my situation. The enemy cannot and will not lead you in all truth. Jesus said it best this way.

John 14:6 "I am the way, the truth, and the life: no man cometh unto the Father, but by me."

Jesus is Lord! Glory to God and in utilizing Jesus as my ticket and my way to God gave me reassurance that I couldn't lose. Jesus is also life to me, everything that we will ever need and seek is in

God, His Son, and precious Holy Spirit. I'm so glad that I decided to choose wisely. Because it states, "No man cometh to the Father, but by me." I have learned that there is no other way. Jesus is the ultimate path to our Father. I absolutely love this.

On the flip side of that I am reminded of this scripture:

John 10:10 "The thief cometh not, but for to steal, and to kill, and to destroy: I come that they might have life and that they might have it more abundantly."

This scripture exemplifies there's no life, truth, or guidance in the enemy. I'm not one to tell you that serving the enemy isn't exciting and sometimes pleasurable. The things of the world often appear to be welcoming. Only to find out later as Adam and Eve did, that things that seem good to us are not necessarily good for us! Some things that look good are dangerous for our journey. We should instead look to please God rather than please our flesh. Our flesh will hunger and thirst after things we should shun. Our spirit is willing, but our flesh becomes weak.

Matthew 26:41 "Watch and pray, that ye enter not into temptation: the spirit indeed is willing, but the flesh is weak."

Matthew 5:6 "Blessed are they which do hunger and thirst after righteousness: for they shall be filled."

Our spirit hungers to do justice but our flesh hunger to do evil and wicked things. Our flesh will cause us to get in messy situations or circumstances to override God's commandments. If this happens, we must flee. STOP! PAUSE! GO IN ANOTHER DIRECTION! In the end, your willingness to please God will be more profitable for your life.

In conclusion of this chapter, God Himself led me to consider this portion of this book. I was led to discuss what led to us getting a CT scan for Justace. Wow, that was the beauty of listening to the voice of God.

Father God, we pray for a willingness to hear you. We pray that as we hear your voice, we will obey your word and walk in obedience to what you are leading us to do and to say. In your Word, Jesus said, I am the way, the truth, and the life! Today we choose His guidance and command for He is the way in Jesus name we pray, Amen.

I remember my Aunt Helen took us to the doctor that morning to get x-rays. Justace was so nervous and kept asking why we had to come here. Although all she had to do was lay there and have pictures taken, she was still hesitant and afraid. It was hard for me to answer all the questions she asked me. "Mommy, why do I have to come here? Mommy, can I please go to school? Mommy, what are they going to do to me? Is it going to hurt today? Mommy, I'm so scared. Mommy I don't want to do this. Please, mommy!" I could only imagine how frightening this experience was for my ten-year-old. I would pray with her of course, and I was always praying under my breath as she was going through all of this. Believing God had already taken care of it. It was something that we had to experience and would get through together. I knew that we could and that we would! I said to myself, this too shall pass!

Now we're at the radiologist's office. The radiologist took x-rays on Day 1 and ordered Justace to come in a second time to look more in-depth. I thought they must be on to something. It was bittersweet for me. Bitter in that something was wrong, and sweet in the regard that we were finally finding the underlying cause of what was going on inside her body. I was so tired at that point. Earlier that week at the pediatric clinic, I had asked the doctor to see a specialist. Her response to me, "Mom, with your kind of insurance, it will take me six months to get it approved."

I want to discuss this portion in the book as well because people need to know that regardless of your present circumstance and what you have or may not have does not determine the outcome of the situation. I could've settled for what the doctor said, but I didn't. Sometimes in life when you desperately need something that your money can't buy, that's when your faith steps in. You must go after what you desire even when it appears and look like you can't. At that time, I didn't have the best insurance, but I served a God that owns the entire world. I wasn't going to take NO for an answer, I needed God to move and open a door for me! Something in me made me believe that this too shall pass!!!

Furthermore, there is another scripture that applies to our lives. "But my God shall supply all your need according to his riches in glory by Christ Jesus" (Philippians 4:19). All our needs are supplied according to His riches in glory by Christ. Every need is covered because our needs are not based upon a financial system but founded in God's order of provision. His system is fail-proof, never goes in recession and cannot be altered. God's system is built to last.

This too shall pass because there is a system more prominent than my circumstance.

Chapter Seven
God Said Let There Be Light, Day One

Understand you may not have all the resources you need to get done what needs to get done but are you willing to open your mouth and ask? According to the doctor, she said it would take months for Justace to get a referral, but it didn't stop me from asking more questions. Don't settle and watch your life wither away but open your mouth and make demands. I remember reading about when the earth was void and full of darkness, God opened his mouth and created things. When He said let there be, then it was. Let's look at Genesis chapter 1.

1 "In the beginning, God created the heaven and the earth." 2 "And the earth was without form, and void, and darkness was upon the face of the deep. And the Spirit of God moved upon the face of the waters." 3 "And God said, Let there be light: and there was light." 4 "And God saw the light, that it was good."

When we look at this passage, it discusses how God created the heaven and the earth. The earth was disorganized and didn't have formation, and it was dark. Now, here is a situation God could have allowed to stay without formality and in darkness. Instead, he opened his mouth and created the world for us to abide in. I could have walked out of the doctor's office and continued living without form and void. But I made a choice to submit my life to formation and validity. At the time, my child was sick and I didn't know what was going on, I needed answers. There's no way I could've sat there in a dark place much longer. I needed things to begin to form in my life. I needed light in my life. It wasn't going to happen with a closed mouth. No, ma'am, I may not have the best insurance, but Jehovah Jireh has me insured. Stop sitting in darkness and pursue the light of God. It's in what you say. Decree a thing and let it be. "Thou shalt also decree a thing, and it shall be established unto thee: and the light shall shine upon thy ways" (Job 22:28). No longer waste time watching things that have not yet formed. Open up your mouth!!!! What happens when we began to speak? People, places, and things around us are affected. For example, if someone ever said something hurtful to you, remember how bad it made you feel versus the time when someone spoke a powerful, loving word to you and how good you felt. A closed mouth produces a continued cycle of stagnation. An opened mouth produces life. Never be underestimated by what others say. Control the atmosphere wherever you are! Own it and create positive outcomes in your life. The spoken Word of God produced light. Let me show you how my response to what the doctor said resulted in light for my life.

I said, "Surely we can do something. I don't want my daughter admitted to the hospital, but I continually massage her stomach….. You said it was stool backed up, that can't be healthy for her body, and shouldn't it be out by now? I said I think she needs to see a specialist of some kind. That's when she responded to me, "Okay mom, I can let her get another X-ray." (Here's the light). Now those words from the doctor, I will never forget because I felt like she just brushed me off in times past. Her body language appeared, "I just want to get her out of my office, she keeps complaining but all it is, is stool and it will eventually come out." I was upset with her and the other doctors because I had come in repeatedly for answers. I was told to exercise her legs and massage her stomach and increase the laxatives for her bowels to move. My feelings of anger had derived from several things, but especially all the feelings of "something isn't right." I believe and know it was God. I kept feeling and thinking something isn't adding up. God had sharpened my discernment. At that time, I just wanted peace and help for my daughter. I didn't want to hear bad news, but I wanted to know what was going on. I do thank God for the unction, I had to keep going and persistently asking questions. I wasn't unlearned as it related to my daughter. By this time, I'm watching her closely. I even took her to a therapist because I would look upon my child and I thought something is going on, God, what is it?" I knew something wasn't right. I charge any parent to always study their child. Parents should be able to know when there is an internal factor trying to take control of their child. These internal factors that were going on released external factors where I would stop and look at my baby for minutes without her knowing. I would observe her actions more, her facial expressions, body language, grades in school, behavior in and outside the home, etc.... Remember my daughter never complained about having pain. She never said, "Mommy, my tummy hurts." Never.... God allowed me to see my child on this scale and for that, I will forever thank him. Thank you, God I love you!

    I would also like to challenge parents, whenever they see their children after school and daycare; they should give them their full attention. Whenever you have been away from your child for any given length of time, whether its work, school, church, or business, you should greet them in the highest regard of love. By doing so, you demonstrate to the child that I have been away from my parents all day, and now that I see them, they are into me. They are concerned about who I am as well as my time. Often parents approach their children, and they are having a conversation on the phone, on social media or frustrated with the kind of day that they had. Guess what, your child does not deserve to greet you, hearing you converse about who shot John or how negative your day was. Let's say your day was terrible; do not bring that to your child. Pull off to the side of the road, go to the park and release that negative energy before you see them or at least, get yourself together before greeting them. Most of all, this gives you an opportunity to be free yourself. Bring powerful positive energy when you greet and embrace them. The point of the matter is taking a moment to fulfill your child's needs by acknowledging them properly after being absent for a few hours or days. Many parents often say: "Well, I don't know when my child changed. I remember one day, he or she wasn't the same anymore. Every time I try to ask questions, they don't respond to me, I can't get them to open up to me." Wow! I've been here myself. It wasn't until I had to examine myself and learn the importance of greetings. Greet your child or children like they are the only ones in the world. Make them feel special. Make them feel relevant to the point that there is always an open portal from you to them. There is still an opening for you to see your child fully and for them to know who you are in their life. But if when we come in from a long day and still occupied, where does that leave the parent-child relationship? Yes, exactly clogged up and cluttered. We must learn to come in with a clear passage for the parent-child relationship, to keep that relationship portal clean and free. This structure allows positive energy to flow endlessly and demonstrates to your child that you love and respect the relationship. This results in them respecting you more. All of this is necessary to understand the importance of and the proper way to greet your child(ren). You can see them clearly; then nothing will come upon you unaware.

So, off we went to the radiologist because I opened my mouth (my light). The first day was okay, but it was the second and third day that would alter the rest of our lives. Let's look further:

It's imperative that you move forward when you get your light, no matter the size of it because even the smallest glare will guide you to the expected end. Because I opened my mouth, I was able to take my daughter to the radiologist, and they performed an X-ray on her. Justace was nervous because of the large equipment and X-rays and having to wear a hospital gown. In my mind, I thought' "It's not that bad." However, for a child to have to experience more doctors' visits other than the norm, is not always easy for them. The look in her eyes was terrifying. My heart went out to her. I remember watching her, praying, and just wondering what is going on and asking God, why are we here? Once the X-rays were completed, they asked us to come back the next day.

Remember when the light comes on, utilize it! God provided me light as He did on day 1 in the book of Genesis. The world would be dark if there weren't any light today. I charge you to speak something that never existed before especially while in a dark place. I was in a very dark place with questions, and so many voids that I needed answered. As God did, so did I. I opened my mouth, and it created a portal for me to begin a journey that only God could've strengthened me to take. Again, don't just sit in dark places waiting for it to fall out of the sky. Whatever IT may be, open up your mouth. Open up your mouth and pray, open up your mouth and talk to people. Open your mouth and speak to the storm until the light comes. Open up your mouth and speak life into your children, businesses, dreams, and visions. Never allow what you have which usually is not enough cause you to stay in darkness. I dare you to speak to it. Understand that once you speak, it begins to change the situation. Know that this too shall pass. Speaking the word and positive declarations will cause us to move through any storm. Words bring activation. This too shall pass!!!

KJV Proverbs 18:21 "Death and life are in the power of the tongue, And those who love it will eat its fruit."

International Standard Version Isaiah 3:10 "Tell the righteous that things will go well because they will enjoy the fruit of their actions."

KJV Colossian 4:6 "Let your speech be always with grace, seasoned with salt, that ye may know how ye ought to answer every man."

New International Version Ephesians 4:29 "Do not let any unwholesome talk come out of your mouths, but only what is helpful for building others up according to their needs, that it may benefit those who listen."

Chapter Eight
Thankful Persistence

We went back to the doctor on day two and this day was a bit different. My daughter was ordered to have more X-rays done. They wanted to see things more in-depth. So, we did. And when it was time for me to speak to the radiologist, I left Justace and her sister in a small room with the nurse. I knew he had something he wanted to say. I could feel it. You must understand I had been in a place of asking God what is going on for weeks and that particular day, I felt like I was getting closer to hearing my answer. The radiologist said to me, "Mom, how did you get here, what led to this point?" I said, "Sir, it may seem strange to you but during January, God spoke to me in my kitchen as I was looking at my daughter and said, "take Justace to the doctor". At the time, I'm watching a beautiful 10-year-old who is acting normal and running around with her little sister Jordin as all little girls do. I looked at her and said Justace, "Are you okay sweetheart." She responds, "yes." I remember exactly where I was when I heard the words. It startled me because I knew what I heard but watching my daughter, it was like nothing can be wrong with her. I didn't take her to the doctor that day. I remember mentioning it to my mother. It was a few days before the Spring of 2016 semester was to start, and I felt the need to take my daughter to the doctor. They examined her, and she mentioned she doesn't use the bathroom as she normally did. I thought what do you mean? Because she was having trouble using the bathroom regularly, and that particular day, the doctors ordered Mira lax for my child." I told the radiologist it seemed like as soon as I started giving her the laxative, it seemed like my daughter bowels locked up on her and got worst. I explained how I would take her back and forth to the doctor and weeks after examining her, all they instructed was laxatives, exercise her legs and massaging the stomach area. I finally told him I practically begged the doctor to see a specialist, but because of my insurance, they said it could take about six months for it to be approved. Then she blurted out, "Okay mom, you can have another X-ray." Now there was an earlier X-ray provided to us, but it only showed stool backed up. So, that's what they thought the only issue was her bowels." The radiologist looked at me and stood up. He said to me, "You ought to thank your God for speaking to you in your kitchen that day, and I want to thank you for being so persistent with your daughter's doctor. He went further to say, "There is something in your daughter's abdomen. Unfortunately, we can't tell what it is, but tomorrow we need you to bring her back in for a CT scan, it's more than bowels. "

I remember nodding my head, and the tears began to flow. Boy oh boy, this was a crying season for me. I don't remember if I said you're welcome because all I could do is wonder what is it, God? What is going on with my baby girl? Is this why I've been on sabbatical since February and intense prayer since January. I remember hearing God say, "rest and pray, do not take any assignment to preach or dance." God, I'm thinking, "What's going on?" I wanted to cry longer, but I couldn't because I had two beautiful girls in the next room waiting for their mommy. Often when you want to cry, you can't because they are right there waiting for you and they need you to be there. I held my tears back, and I couldn't wait for the next day to come. I don't recommend this to anyone. When you need to cry- do it. Take a moment to release and cleanse yourself. At this moment, on day two, I had to realize, the light I received the day before got me to this point. I opened my mouth, now I was getting answers. It was as if I was in another world wondering where exactly am I and what is this in my baby's belly. I got the contrast that was needed for my daughter's CT scan the next day, and I walked away knowing that this too shall pass!

Day two in the book of Genesis, God created the firmament.

Genesis 2:6 "And God said, "Let there be a firmament in the midst of the waters, and let it divide the waters from the waters." 7 "And God made the firmament, and divided the waters which were under the firmament from the waters which were above the firmament: and it was so. 8 And God called the firmament Heaven. And the evening and the morning were the second day."

When we examined the word firmament, derived from the Hebrew word *Raquiya* meaning expanse -a visible arch of the sky. Day two for Justace and I was the fact that something became visible to us. We now understood that there was something there far beyond bowels being backed up. When we further examine the word "expanse," it is the distance from which something has the ability for expansion. In the Greek firmament is *"stereoma"* meaning a firm or solid structure. The mass that was now visible in Justace's belly was the size of a 4-pound ball and had spread in other places in her abdomen and other female organs.

God lead me to examine the creation of the earth and my daughter's diagnoses together. In parallel on day two, in the book of Genesis a firmament is made visible and day two for us, a mass is visible for us to see by way of X-ray. God called the firmament heaven, and the Radiologist called what was in Justace abdomen a mass. But this too shall pass. I didn't understand the intensity of the mass, but I knew that this mass was going to pass.

Mark 13:31 "Heaven and earth shall pass away: but my words shall not pass away."

My point: things can pass away, and please, know that it will, and it is going to happen. The only thing that will stand is the Word. That's why it's imperative that we open our mouths and not speak foolishly and loosely. But we are to speak the word. I had to declare the Word of God because only the word was going to last over my situation. To some, getting the news that there is a mass in the belly of a child can be very challenging and heartbreaking.

Receiving the report of anything negative can dampen your spirit, but don't stay there; speak the word over your situation, live and get up. A relationship can fall apart; you may get fired from a job, that business may not prosper, but the one thing you can bank on is the Word of God. Although I didn't want to hear there was a mass in Justace's belly, I knew that I could speak the word of God over it and it had to go. It was already imperative that I had increased my prayer life during that season, and I had already commanded what was in her belly to go. Now God had allowed me to see a mass; it was my responsibility to speak the word. Declare the Word because when all else fails, the word of God is going to stand and see us through. I couldn't go back at this point because it's the Word that I have hidden in my heart that I will not sin as the Bible states. I have the word of God in me that causes me to triumph and not fail!

Psalm 199:11 "Thy word have I hid in mine heart, that I might not sin against thee."

I can't sin and go back now because the word will elevate me amid what I'm facing. I have the word of God stored up on the inside, and I can now utilize it and declare what I need in my life. I'm not going out like that! I refuse to. When we are true believers and have the word of God, we can use it at any given moment to conquer anything. The thing about storms that we encounter is, we don't know how long they are going to last, but we can depend on God and His word. There is substance and power in the Word. The Bible says (by the way I love this scripture):

Hebrews 4:12 "For the word of God is quick, and powerful, and sharper than any two-edged sword, piercing even to the dividing asunder of soul and spirit, and of the joints and marrow, and is a discerner of the thoughts and intents of the heart."

The word can go where you can't go. Not to get ahead of myself but, I remember commenting, "I wish I could take that mass out of my baby myself." Well, guess what? I can by praying and speaking the word. Some people will miss it. Please don't let it be you. Remember Day 1, God said let there be light and boom it happened! The words commanded activation for something to be created. When you get bad news, speak the word and let it begin activation for healing, miracles, creations, breakthroughs, avenues, portals, businesses, books, homes, schools, and prosperity in your life. Of course, in my situation, I had to declare the word as it relates to healing, miracles, and deliverance, so I gathered scriptures of healing, miracles, and deliverance. If you need your car repaired, you're not going to go to the ice cream shop. No, you're going to take your car to the best mechanic to get the job done. You will only go to the ice cream shop to eat ice cream. When you have an infirmity, you need deliverance, and you need a miracle. When you are sick, you need healing. When you experience brokenness, you need to gain wholeness. Gather scripture that relates to your situation. What's beautiful about the world we live in today is the fact that we can go online and Google this information. If you need scriptures to come out of poverty, simply type in the search bar "scriptures for prosperity." My favorite Bible to read is the King James Version. (I sometimes read other versions for clarity and insight). Utilize the word to get through your situation. Say it out loud until you see the results of it! The word and the Bible is the ultimate guide in life.

God's word holds Him accountable. God will not violate his word. Whatever God speaks becomes law; therefore, God becomes trapped by what He says. The Father cannot lie so if His word commands that we are already healed, then so be it, healing is our portion (Isaiah 53:5). If God states in His word according to Jeremiah 29:11, "that He knows the thoughts that he thinks towards us and has a plan and a purpose for our life", and regardless of a jacked-up life God still has a plan and a purpose.

Psalm 119:105 "Thy word is a lamp unto my feet, and a light unto my path."

There's no way you can have the Word as a part of your life and not see the results of it. Not only will you hear the word but you will be a doer of the word.

Chapter Nine
Foundations

D_{ay 3}

Genesis 1: 9 "And God said, Let the waters under the heaven be gathered together unto one place, and let the dry land appear: and it was so." 10 "And God called the dry land Earth; the gathering together of the waters called the Seas: and God saw that it was good." 11 "And God said, Let the earth bring forth grass, the herb yielding seed, and the fruit tree yielding fruit after his kind, whose seed is in itself, upon the earth: and it was so."

On this day, the dry ground appeared which represents a foundation to walk on. No longer was it just water, but the dry ground was created to provide an avenue to walk upon and have a sense of stability. The third day of finding out what was going on with my daughter allowed me to have a foundation to navigate to our next move. Let's discuss our third day with the radiologist: March 11th, 2016, we went to the doctor, and Justace was disgusted already that I withheld her from school all week. She was concerned about missing school work, her teachers, and her friends. She cried and begged me not to keep her out so many days. That week I had increased her laxatives, and I knew that going to school wouldn't be the best idea. She was using the restroom quite frequently, everything she drank ran right through her, yet her stomach was hard.

As her mother, I had to make the decision. I am thankful to have a child that wanted to go to school. Some children cry because they have to go. She was in tears because she had to stay home. So, on the morning of the 11th, we focused on drinking the contrast for her CT scans. It was difficult for her trying to get it down, but she did it. I remember watching her do things that the doctors ordered for over a process of months! All I can say is The Lord was with my child. Justace demonstrated strength to me on so many levels. I watched her laugh, cry, get frustrated, giggle, and get so restless, but she would always do what was necessary. I must pause and say thank you, Lord! I appreciate the Lord for each day. I thank Him for all the hard days and the days I had to be strengthened to help her. She needed me more than ever so I needed to keep the drive and motivation to get through each phase of this challenge.

Once we arrived, Justace still had some contrast left, but the team decided she had digested enough to proceed with the CT scans. They started an IV. I remember thinking this was a lot for a ten-year-old little girl to experience. Jordin and I watched from the other room as she completed her scans; she was so frightened. I stayed in as long as they would allow. Then I would go into the next room. But every chance I had to go in and hold hands with my baby, I would! She cried and looked at me so anxiously like, "Mommy what's happening to me and why am I here?" I would respond, "Sweetie we're just taking pictures of you so we can see what's in your stomach, so we'll know what to do. I know you're tired, and I am too, but baby let's get this done so we can get all this behind us. Mommy is here with you. Jordin and I are not going to leave you. I love you, baby." As I walked into the next room, she hesitantly released my hand. It was a hurtful thing watching my little girl cry. I can still see the look on her face. It makes me sometimes cry just thinking about it.

I remember that day, getting dropped off because the two vehicles I owned at the time were older and couldn't pass inspection. In the state of North Carolina, if the check engine light is on, the car will not pass inspection. I had cars, but I couldn't use them. On that particular day, I had a dear friend drop us off. When it was time to leave, my sister came to pick us up. I wasn't going to leave without speaking to the Radiologist. As I walked my children outside, the nurse followed us out and stated: "Mom, please don't leave we need to talk to you." Although I knew it was something, I didn't know the magnitude. I said, "They are leaving, I'm not." She said, "Great, the doctor wants to speak to you." I'm thinking, "of course, this is what I've been waiting for." We both walked inside, and I sat in the chair in front of a different doctor than I had the day before. When I sat down, this old man sat up in his seat to grasp my FULL ATTENTION. He leans in real close to me. He said, "Mom, you have a journey ahead of you. What I'm looking at with your daughter is very rare. Your little girl needs a specialist, and she needs one as soon as possible." At this point, I am crying, listening, and thinking I begged her doctor for a specialist for weeks. He went further to say, "We are trying to reach her doctor for you to get to Duke." He said, "We believe there is a large tumor in her abdomen, but it's too large for us to tell. We have never seen anything like this for the age of your daughter. Mom, you will get through this." I said, "Sir, I need to go find her doctor now so I can take my baby to Duke I have to go!!!"

Like the third day when God created dry ground, this provided an open portal to navigate and get to other places. I knew that the Mira lax was not the answer to my daughter's condition and talking with a specialist will lead me to results. The radiologist confirmed I was right. There's nothing like a mothers whose right. Now, I am without a car because my sister had just left to take my daughters to eat, and I began to walk to the doctor's office. I made a call to the office, but could not get an answer, so I left a voicemail. On the way, the doctor called me back immediately and said, "Mom, I got your message, and I am writing the referral for the specialist now." Of course, she's writing it!! I had told her beforehand, that's what we needed, a referral weeks ago!!

Sometimes, when you ask for things in life, you may not get the results you're seeking right away, but trust and know that your words have power and they are working for you. Your words have power, and they are working for you! You may or may not get an immediate response, but never stop pursuing what God has placed in your heart. Unfavorable responses may come but know this too shall pass. There have been times that many of us have pursued so many goals, dreams, and visions and sought other people in particular positions that could help us, only to get a "no," I can't; or this can take months, maybe years, or it's impossible. I have come to learn people make choices that are beneficial to them. I understand doctors have protocol, policies, and procedures, but understand God can override all policies, protocols, and procedures. I am a reflection of His likeness; I can override policies, protocols, and procedures. So again, don't allow your desires and wants to diminish because of people. I battled with the thought as it related to her doctors, "If this were their child, they would have done something differently; that's exactly how I feel, and I won't change that. My only option was my faith in God, and I finally got what I needed. Wow, serving God is the best thing that has happened to me! My faith in Him keeps a consistent drive within me because the results of serving Him and having faith are amazing. What do I mean by this, God will open up portals and blessings for which you don't qualify! There are benefits to serving God.

Psalm 103: 1 "Bless the LORD, O my soul: and all that is within me, bless his holy name." 2 "Bless the LORD, O my soul, and forget not all His benefits." 3 "Who forgiveth all thine iniquities; who healeth all thy diseases." 4 "Who redeemeth thy life from destruction; who crowneth thee with lovingkindness and tender mercies; 5 Who satisfieth thy mouth with good things; so that thy youth is renewed like the eagle's."

Verse 2 said, "forget not all his benefits. Yes, there are benefits in honoring and blessing the Lord. I'm sure we could all utilize the benefits of the Lord. Don't waste your benefits but allow them to work in your favor."

I took pleasure in this scripture as well:

Psalm 68: 19 "Blessed be the Lord, who daily loadeth us with benefits, even the God of our salvation. Selah."

When we see the word "Selah", we must stop and think about it, and ponder a little while. It says "Blessed be the Lord, who daily loadeth us with benefits." This passage describes an ongoing cycle of reward. Not just when you decide to do something great for God. His word says "He's daily loading us with benefits." God knows how to handle and take care of His people.

Psalm 116: 12 "What shall I render unto the LORD for all His benefits toward me?" 13 "I will take the cup of salvation, and call upon the name of the LORD."

This verse asks a question. I often look at questions in the Bible as a kind indicator for us to take heed especially when it provides us the answer. The Psalm explains that because God is loading us with benefits, we will take the cup of salvation, and call upon the name of the Lord. What is the cup of salvation? Here salvation is derived from the Hebrew word "*Yeshuah*", meaning saved, delivered, aid, victory, prosperity, health, help, and welfare. Another important factor I have come to learn is whenever a question arises, we are forced to deal with what's on the inside of us.

If you are reading this book, it would be rude for me not to offer salvation unto you. Often with the cares of the world, we forget about our relationship with God, the importance and the benefits of salvation. If you are in a backslidden condition or don't know God as you should and want to give your life to Him, please read the prayer of salvation and find a word-based church where you can go and grow into a kingdom citizen. Whenever I minister, I tell people I'm coming in the name of the Lord and my only agenda is salvation, rededication, and elevation. 'Salvation' for many of us who need to surrender to God, 'Rededication' for those who have lost their way and are in a backslidden state and 'Elevation' for those who are in right standing with God but desire to go to another dimension, place, or level with Him because as believers, we should aim to increase in Him.

A prayer of salvation......

Father, I ask you to forgive me for my sins, and I ask you to create in me a clean heart and renew a right spirit on the inside of me. I invite you in and welcome you into my spirit, soul, and body. Lead and guide me into all truth. Save me and deliver me out of a world of sin. I believe Jesus is the son of God and according to the Word, He is the way, the truth, and the life and no man cometh to the Father except by Him. I surrender my will to your will in Jesus name, Amen.

If you have prayed this prayer, seek God for the right church, the right pastors, and allow Him to lead you and to guide you.

I believe we left off discussing the phone call where the doctor was writing the referral form for Justace to go to Duke. By this time, my sister had come back to pick me up, so I didn't have to walk the whole way. Of course, when I got in the car, my daughter asked, "Mommy, what did they say about me." I said, "Baby let's go over to the pediatric clinic and get some paperwork. They are going to let us see a specialist. That way, this thing they see in your tummy can be removed." "Well, Mommy what is it?" I said, "Sweetie I don't know, but the specialist will help us." I remember tons of questions and not enough answers. The only thing that I could feel was the excruciating pain that was going through my body — the pressure in my face from the tears that I held in. Then the minor relief when I was able to let a tear out and quickly wiped my face before my children could see. The myriad of thoughts running through my mind concerning the journey ahead was trying to overtake me.

Meanwhile, my sister is asking, "Candace, what is wrong?" I couldn't respond because my babies were in the car. I only remember the weight of the pressure and so much pain. I just wanted to scream at the top of my lungs and release all the heaviness I was feeling.

I arrived, and the doctor gave me the paperwork. She really couldn't look me in my eyes, but at that moment, I couldn't ponder on that. I knew she felt terrible. She did, however, embrace my daughter and me and said she would be praying for us. At this point, it was unbelievable to everyone. How do you go from bowels being backed up to a large mass/tumor in her abdomen? I don't hate that particular doctor's office; I believe they failed us. They failed us big time. I think they could have made better decisions. Doctors felt her stomach during each examination, but yet, we were sent home each time. There were times I would "walk-in" and ask why do I still feel the stool?" I can still see the reactions and facial expressions. "Oh, mom, that's just stool, just give it some time and it will eventually go away, she's pretty backed up."

But moving forward, she gave me the paperwork and called Duke to inform them of our coming. She informed us that she didn't know how long we would be there, but we needed to pack a bag. I called to tell my mother and my extended family who would care for my youngest daughter.

I walked into my home with so much on my mind. I went upstairs, and I began to pack our bags. Her father and I didn't talk as much, but I knew I had to make that phone call. It seems every other time I took her to the physician, I didn't need to contact him because it wasn't an emergency. This time it was entirely different. I was accustomed to being Supermom and handling it on my own, but this time I had to involve him. This time, Justace being sick wasn't a common cold or an eye infection. I couldn't just give her eye drops or cold medicine. This situation was far beyond what I ever imagined. But the greatest thing I can say out of all of this is, in January, God instructed me to take Justace to the doctor. I remember it just as plain as day. Now, God with His awesomeness wouldn't speak to me without leading me after the fact. Remember, I stated earlier that His word would not fail Him or us. His words have substance. If He led me, THEN undoubtedly, He will lead me NOW. Candace, take Justace to the doctor," were the words God spoke to me early January standing in my kitchen. He was with me then and He was still with me.

Day 1, let there be light (my light was getting to the radiologist) Day 2, let there be a firmament (radiologist saw the mass) and Day 3, God provided dry ground (a firm foundation to get to the specialist in order to get the mass out). This book is a blessing to me. I often stop because I cry thinking about the goodness of the Lord. I cry because writing is like reliving it. It's like I can feel certain things. Could this be why the Bible instructs us to write the vision and make it plain? Some of us are walking around with so much vision inside and never take a moment to write it out. When you write your vision, you can feel the results of it. When you take the time to write what's on the inside of you, other things begin to unfold and come out of you that you didn't know. Take the time to write out your dreams and goals. The Bible states Habakkuk 2:1 "I will stand upon my watch, and set me upon the tower, and will watch to see what he will say unto me, and what I shall answer when I am reproved." 2 "And the LORD answered me, and said, Write the vision, and make it plain upon tables, that he may run that readeth it." 3 "For the vision is yet for an appointed time, but at the end, it shall speak, and not lie: though it tarry, wait for it; because it will surely come, it will not tarry."

Write the vision and make it plain that he may run that readeth it. That "he" can be others around you or that he can be "you." Could it be you need to write out your vision for you to run with it? Or do you want it to settle around in your mind without the results? It is highly impossible to have a successful vision without writing it out. Every powerful church, business, or entity has a mission statement, objective, and plan. You will never purchase anything from a business without them giving you instructions and information about the company. How would you feel if the next time you buy something, and it's not packaged with information about the company name? We feel comfortable making purchases when we know the policies, procedures, and protocols are inside.

Without them, we don't know how to utilize the product. Many of us are products to many people, places, and things. Without people being able to understand our vision, they will not send for us. Vision helps you identify yourself. Wow, how did I get here? I know this book was purchased by some people who seek guidance on how to get past situations. But understand this, writing out your vision in the midst of hell and disadvantages will better prove how great you really are.

The Bible says, "When we're weak, that's when we're strong." I said to myself, Paul how did you come up with this one. Come with me.

2 Corinthians 12:8 "For this thing, I besought the Lord thrice, that it might depart from me." 9 "And he said unto me, My grace is sufficient for thee: for my strength is made perfect in weakness. Most gladly, will I rather glory in my infirmities, that the power of Christ may rest upon me." 10 "Therefore, I take pleasure in infirmities, in reproaches, in necessities, in persecutions, in distresses for Christ's sake: for when I am weak, then am I strong."

Paul wanted the thorn removed from his flesh. But God refused and said no, my grace is sufficient and my strength is made perfect in weakness. Thus, when Paul learned this, he said well now, most gladly, I will rather glory in my infirmities that the power of Christ may rest upon me. In other words, Lord, I will glorify you in the midst of this because this shows you I understand that my strength is made perfect in you. Although I am weak right now, I choose to tap into who you are, because your grace is sufficient for me. Furthermore, we need the power of Christ to produce our purpose. We need the pain to produce the greater us.

1 Corinthians 6: 14 "And God hath both raised up the Lord, and will also raise up us by his own power." 15 "Know ye not that your bodies are the members of Christ?"

There are times it takes storms and trials for us to see the power of Christ. Yes, because often when things are going well, we can't see if we are humble. When our lives are going as planned, and nothing is wrong or bothering us, we forget and start going through the motions.

Sometimes, we don't pray as we should, come to church, fast, live a holy or righteous life. But once we find ourselves in a storm, we get on our knees. The beautiful thing about that is the power of Christ will come and rest upon us. Now we have the strength to endure and make it, knowing that this too shall pass!! Some things won't leave right? Then, when we pray. Case in point, this passage with Paul, he understood that when this happened, God's grace was sufficient for him. It won't kill you; it will only make you stronger. The storm won't last always; I repeat, this too shall pass!

Now back to the story. I am at home packing, and my family is deciding who's going to travel with me. My fiancé at the time is demanding that I take his car. I said, "No I can't leave you without a vehicle!" He was reminding me to call his dad. So know all this is running through my mind. You must understand that no one woke up that morning expecting me to say we have to drive to Duke and spend a few days because Justace is very sick. Everyone was trying to help me get situated and prepared for the next few days. As I was preparing to head to Duke, I begin to think about things I needed to do.

I had to make the call to inform my daughter's dad and his family about what was going on. That was the first time I had to call him and utter that something was wrong. For five years, he had resided in another city, and I pretty much had a handle on things. I didn't get an answer, but I left voicemails. On our way, I held my daughter in the backseat until we got to Duke. It was a different kind of ride going there. I felt like I was leaving for a long time. I felt like I was leaving something behind. You ever had to take a trip and didn't really know what was happening. It felt like I was having an out-of-body experience. It was a trip that made me secretly cry. Yep, those trips when you don't know what to expect, all you know is I have to take this trip….. That's how I felt, I didn't know what was ahead, but I was going with God on my mind.

When we arrived at Duke University Medical Center, there were so many people waiting. I checked in, and they saw our information in the system and got us to the back quickly. We stayed in the ER for a few hours and met a pediatric doctor (Dr. Michael) who I must say was excellent. I will say that Duke has some of the best doctors around and they made my daughter and our family feel welcome. It's like they knew what to say. They informed us that because it was the weekend, it wouldn't be until Monday until they could look at what was inside her belly. They gave us a room on the 5300 hall, and we went to bed.

Sometime later, in the wee hours of the night, Justace's dad arrived. I remember waking up, looking at the ceiling. I took a deep breath and examined the room. My mother was sleeping in the recliner, her dad was on the floor, and I was in bed with Justace. I looked up and said, God, "Why am I here?" and I asked God, "How did I end up in this small hospital room with someone who caused me so much pain." I went back to sleep holding my baby. Oh, she began to get a lot of love from mommy. I honestly was so used to embracing my youngest because she was the baby. But now Justace was pulling on me and wrapping my arms around her, and frankly, it felt good. I was honored to hold my daughter and be with her every step of the way.

Chapter Ten
You Made A Way

Day 4 and Day 5

These two days consisted of so much. What a weekend it was at Duke University Medical Center! On Day 4, it was a Saturday, a team of doctors greeted us that morning. They confirmed that there was a tumor in Justace's belly from viewing the x-rays. They allowed us to get a visual of the mass. I remember also blanking out because I couldn't believe what I was seeing and how large this tumor was. I know that this tumor must've been growing for months, maybe years. It was like I was in space or something. Her dad, my sister, brother-in-law, and I watched the X-ray, and we cried listening to the doctors talk to us about it. My mother was kind enough to stay in the room with Justace. We decided to listen to what the doctors had to say first and then, discuss the needed information with Justace later. Once again, the team of physicians made Justace feel very comfortable. They told us they would perform surgery on Monday and remove the tumor from her body. They told us to relax; it would be a long weekend. I remember wiping the tears from my face before going back into the room. Justace was already stressed enough, and I could not bring any more stress on her. At least, this is how I felt at that time. I didn't know if it was okay to cry or not. I didn't want her to be stressed out or fearful any more than she already was. We went back into the room and just got as comfortable as we could. We prayed so much during that time. I woke up and played Travis Greene's song, "You made a way." I prophetically played the song on purpose. That song signified that God made a way for us before we knew what was ahead.

This Too Shall Pass

In the book of Genesis, on day 4, God created the sun, moon, and stars. Right now, all I say is when I saw the x-ray of Justace stomach, I felt like I was in space, it reminded me of the movies or cartoons when someone gets knocked out, and all they can see are stars. That's what that day was like for me. Something hit me, and all I could see were stars. But God, I thank you for the light. You know the sun was created to divide the day and the moon to provide light to the night. I needed a spiritual light in the morning, and I needed a spiritual light in the evening. God became my light this day, and I eventually made it through. Our family filled the room. Whenever you find yourself in a problematic storm, and people take the time to be there with you, that becomes priceless. Then, a host of other people came in. People begin supporting, sending cards and most of all prayers.

I discovered that not everyone that was with me at the beginning of my storm lasted till the end. You look up, and you're alone. You look for them to be there, and they are nowhere around. The storms are sometimes meant to shake up relationships to the point that you will know who is with you and who is not.

Storms will blow in your life, and this may not mean the people don't love you, but that their season may be over in your life. A real storm will bring about changes in relationships. It's part of the process. You think about it in the natural sense. When hurricanes pass, and people have to relocate, maybe forever or maybe for a season, they are forced to live in hotels, with family and friends. During Hurricane Matthew in 2016, my father, Dennis allowed people he didn't know to live with him for a season, all because these people were flooded out and didn't have any place to go. Wow, my dad has always been one of a kind. He's an intelligent man.

But my point from earlier is that my family was right there, they didn't leave our side. Other people did, but my family stayed right there, and God introduced me to other people with our best interests. From the intense day of coming to Duke until days later after the surgery, we prayed and worshipped and believed God that this too shall pass! Whenever you are going through a storm, you will need the right people close to you. You're at a time in your life where you need real intercessors interceding for you. I'm talking about people that will pray as if they are you and evoke God to move for you. Intercessors become you by way of the spirit to pray fervently. You don't need any weak prayers during intense seasons, but you need people around you who are wise and who can get a prayer through.

Day 5 was Sunday! This day was a blessing to us. The doctors made their rounds and often asked Justace if she needed anything or had any questions. She would often reply with, "No, I just want to go home." She will look at me when she says this and would cry. Oooh, this got me every time! I didn't like my baby feeling sad. I don't know about many of you but when my children got sick with the cold, a virus, ear infection, or strep throat, I didn't like to see that, so you can imagine how challenging it was to watch my child in this state. It was Sunday, and everyone knows how much I love going to the house of God. I love having my personal prayer time, but I also enjoy fellowshipping with the saints.

I enjoy worship, the word, and giving. Wow, worship is a spiritual wash, the Word is needed for daily living, and giving provides an opportunity for me to prosper and have more added unto me. Therefore, we asked the doctors if it would be okay to leave and go to church, and they agreed since the surgery was the next day and there was nothing else to do. We got dressed and went to the World Overcomers. My sister resides in Durham, and this is her home church. I remember when we used to take a drive there in times past just to fellowship because the services were so powerful and influential. The church is indescribable!

Psalm 133: 1 "Behold, how good and how pleasant it is for brethren to dwell together in unity!" 2 "It is like the precious ointment upon the head, that ran down upon the beard, even Aaron's beard: that went down to the skirts of his garments;" 3 "As the dew of Hermon, and as the dew that descended upon the mountains of Zion: for there the LORD commanded the blessing, even life for evermore."

It is a good thing for brethren to dwell together in unity. No, everyone will not always agree or get along, but at least, you can agree to disagree. Besides, it's awesome to bring your children up in the things of God. Singing, dancing, serving, and having spiritual outlets in the house of God can be and will be very beneficial. I remember I started dancing at the age of eight, and I am still a minister of dance today at 32. I have been ushered into the prophetic ministry of dance and blessed to minister in places people can only imagine. What if my mother had not guided me in the things of God? Where would I be? What about the conferences that so many people both young and old would've missed? I guess we'll never know why because I found my passion in the house of the Lord, and I ran with it even into my adult age. Some young people don't have anything to look forward to in ministry. (Oh my-this is another topic in another book.)

But another thing I enjoyed about this scripture is this simple yet profound statement, "for there the Lord commanded the blessing even life for evermore" (Psalm 133:3). Now that in itself should make us become unified in the house of the Lord. For there, in unity, the Lord commanded the blessing. The blessing is commanded towards us when we are united. Can you stand to be blessed? I sincerely thank God for a praying mother that instilled the word of God in me. My mom is diligent in whatever she sets her hands to do. She's a hard worker and always strives to help us in any way she can. She's always right there. She has, without a doubt, instilled a place in my heart that leads to being a woman of virtue and a woman of honor. I love my mother so very much.

There are some parents out there right now that are influenced by previous church hurt and abandonment and are making their children suffer by not taking them to church. I honor my mother this day for her persistence in bringing us up the correct way. Did we stray? Yes, we did, but look at where my sisters, brother and I are today. We are all saved and love the Lord. The church is the place to be! The church may not be perfect but guess what, there is no perfect church. I often wonder why people look for the church to be perfect when it's a place for people to come for healing, deliverance and to receive the word. Find a new church if need be, if God leads you to do so. He may guide you to be a repairer of that ministry. Pray about it and consult heavyweights in the gospel. Consult those who demonstrate a passion for God and His people. Don't allow the hurt from an immature person in the church whether it's the pastor or the disciples to determine whether you're going to serve the Lord or not. That's a trick of the enemy.

Proverbs 22:6 "Train up a child in the way he should go: and when he is old, he will not depart from it."

After church, we went out to eat. Then, we took Justace to Frankie's. She played with her cousins, and we rode go-carts. We weren't sure what was ahead of us, but we wanted to enjoy our last day before surgery. The children were happy, running around and having a great time. Justace was finally ready to go back to the hospital. I imagine she had so many questions about what was to come. Here it is, a ten-year-old girl is facing surgery tomorrow. What does all this really mean for her? I can imagine what was going on in her mind from the way she asked me certain things. Also, observing her this particular day, she was in and out. Meaning she would be laughing and playing, then she would have an intent, curious look. I just wanted her to be happy. I just wanted it all to go away. After a fun day, we packed up and went back to the hospital. When we came back to Duke, more of the family had arrived, and they too purchased hotel rooms to be with us during surgery. There's nothing like support.

Chapter Eleven
Let Us Make Man In Our Image

H<small>APPY BIRTHDAY CANDACE</small>

Day 6

Genesis 1: 26 "And God said, Let us make man in our image, after our likeness: and let them have dominion over the fish of the sea, and over the fowl of the air, and over the cattle, and over all the earth, and over every creeping thing that creepeth upon the earth." 27 "So God created man in his own image, in the image of God created he him; male and female created he them." 28 "And God blessed them, and God said unto them, Be fruitful, and multiply, and replenish the earth, and subdue it: and have dominion over the fish of the sea, and over the fowl of the air, and over every living thing that moveth upon the earth."

Day 6 of our journey was my birthday and surgery for Justace. I was born on March 14, 1984, and Day 6 was March 14, 2016. I turned 32 years young and let's just say this wasn't the most exciting day for me. In Genesis, it reads, "So God created man in his own image, in the image of God, created he him; male and female created he them, in verse 28, He gave us dominion." The word dominion comes from the Hebrew word *Radah;* it means to tread down, to prevail against, reign, bear, rule, make to rule, rule over and to take. Now, this is what God has instructed us to have over all the earth. In the book of Jeremiah God said, "Before I formed you in thy mother's belly I knew you, and I had a plan and purpose for your life." So March 14, 1984, became an entryway for me to fulfill why I was born. When I arrived, I was already blessed and given dominion over everything on the earth. My being here was important to God and everything that I was ever going to face in life, God had already equipped me to handle it. Okay, let's go a little deeper. Because I belong to God and represent who He is, I am a product of Him. I did not ask to be here. Out of millions of other sperm cells, I was the one who won. I understand that I came from my mother's womb a winner. Once I was released by God, I came equipped for whatever life was going to bring me.

On Day 6, we were preparing for surgery, and although I had undergone surgery a few times in my life, the feelings I felt for my child were very different. She was very nervous, and we prayed with her and said absolutely everything I could think of that would uplift and encourage her. I told her that when she woke up, I would be right there. It was so surprising that when her father took pictures of us right before she went into surgery, an Angel appeared in the photograph. There have been powerful moments in my life where Angels were captured in pictures especially when I was ministering in dance. This time when I was ministering to my baby, an Angel appeared over the both of us. When her dad showed me the picture, I thought, wow, God you did it again. I always pray and send my Angels on assignment.

Father, in the name of Jesus, I pray that every angel assigned to my life is at work for me. I send them now to stand watch to contend with me and work in my favor. Father, I pray for the angels assigned to me for this situation to be with me today. Your word states, "You've given the angels charge over me to keep me in all my ways." Father, I thank you that my angels are charged and ready in Jesus name.

I remember us talking about the angel in the picture. It did give me peace; I remember hugging and kissing Justace. Although she was still resistant about the surgery, the medicine eventually kicked in, and they rolled her away.

Chapter Twelve
Don't Stay Stuck

Oh my! What a wait it was. I knew that I was going to be in meditation and prayer in the waiting area. I was so ready to see my baby as soon as they wheeled her away. Surgery would take a few hours, and I knew it was going to be a while. So we sat there, I remember people trying to get me to eat. I'm looking at them like I'm not going anywhere; my baby is on the other side having surgery. In my mind, I'm thinking are you all crazy, I'm not leaving my daughter to go eat. I didn't have an appetite anyway. I understand now they knew I needed food. But honestly, at that moment, I needed God. I needed strength just to wait for my daughter.

So after almost two hours, I decided to walk near the doorway to where Justace was having surgery, and I'm standing there, and the surgeon walked out the door. I knew I felt an urge to get up and walk, but I had no idea that Dr. Rice would come out of the procedure room because he still had maybe two hours left. I looked at him and said, "Hey Dr. Rice." I'm thinking, "What in the world is he doing out so soon?" Then I'm thinking about how God lead me to the door, and now he's walking out of it. One thing I love about my relationship with God is He always pricks my spirit about critical moments. I can never explain it, but God deals with me in a particular way. Even how He instructed me to take my daughter to the doctor before she could even complain about anything. Here we stand, Dr. Rice and I. He said, "Hi mom. I want you to know you have a resilient little girl in the room. She's doing excellent. Is your family here with you?" I said, "Yes, they are sitting on the other end." He said, "Well, let's walk over with them." I said, "Okay." I'm thinking as we're walking, "what in the world!" I sat in my chair, and Dr. Rice begins to talk to us. He said, "Well, the surgery is halfway complete. We've gotten to the tumor, but I want you to understand this tumor has become very aggressive. It has spread to different parts of her body, and because of the aggressiveness on her left ovary, we had to remove it." He went further to say more, but his next few words just birthed so much pain on the inside of me. It was like someone came and told me all of your family was involved in an accident and nobody made it out. Those next few words changed the rest of my life. And I can't apologize to anyone who is looking for me to be super-spiritual because I can't be that person for you. I was in pain. I was hurting, and it was like I became sick. I do understand that the enemy wanted me to turn from God and throw in the towel. All kinds of emotions and thoughts ran through me. I've met some people that when they were told some bad news, they shouted and praised God in advance and remained in a good mood. Well, not I! I didn't shout or praise. I just had my faith in God. I didn't have a desire to move. I was stuck in the chair as tears began to roll down my face. The pain I felt within myself began to intensify, and I just cried until I couldn't cry anymore, and my nose ran until it couldn't run anymore. Justace wasn't around me, and I had an opportunity to let it all out! Those around me began to wipe my nose and eyes. I remember being held by those around me. They started praying and doing whatever they felt would be beneficial to me, you name it they did it. They did whatever was necessary to get me from my bending position on the floor. I found myself on the floor because the doctor said, "The only likelihood of your daughter living is through having chemotherapy." Her father spoke up and said, "So it's cancer?!?!" And the doctor softly said, "Yes it is"

I don't remember anything else after that. Just hurt. Oh, you talking about pain! I thought I had already experienced pain on its greatest scale during my early to mid-twenties. I figured I had found pain from previous church hurts and scandals. I thought I saw pain when my parents' divorced. I figured I felt pain when I miscarried over and over again. Oh, I thought I felt pain when someone raped me outside my house in an abandoned vehicle. I thought running inside and taking a shower would get rid of it. Oh no, I thought I found pain when I was left abandoned living in Virginia. I thought I felt pain many times in my life, but the pain of hearing my daughter had cancer was by far the worst pain I ever experienced. And I don't underestimate any of the other painful experiences I dealt with in life, but trust me and hear me, this new pain became the worst pain. Each level of pain has different feelings associated with it. I was hurting so bad that I began to say, "God why is this happening to me? I am living the best way I know how. God, what did I do wrong?" I begin to blame myself and think about all kinds of negative thoughts. I was descending into a dangerous and unhealthy place. About two hours later, a nurse came out talking to me about the port implant in my daughter for chemotherapy treatments. I just cried again. Those words dampened my spirit. Then another nurse came out and said, "Justace is out of surgery, and she's asking for her mommy. Whose Justace mother?"

Wait now; I'm at a place where I decided to give up and die. I was sitting in a seat where the pain had come to paralyze me. I was in a position where self-blame became a factor. I sat in a place where I questioned God. I sat in a place where it appeared everything I thought I knew, I no longer knew them. I was in a situation where negative voices belittled and underestimated me. I was sitting in a valley of decision. I had my faith because I love God. These things came to suffocate who God had already equipped me to be. God had already given me the dominion and authority I needed to make it through anything. Some of us remain in the same location we were at when we discovered the bad news. Some people are still hurting today because of something that happened twenty years ago, and mentally, they have never gotten up from that spot. Some people were well on their way, and life happened, and now, they are discouraged and lifeless.

At that very moment, the pain seemed unbearable, but I had to reach within myself to see a Greater God. A Greater God, bigger than my current circumstance because I had a daughter that I had promised that I would be there for her when she came out of surgery. The nurse said, "Who is Justace's mom? She's asking for her. We just put her in ICU." I got myself up, and I proceeded towards my child. I said a prayer within myself, "God give me the strength to get to my baby. Strengthen me to be what I need to be for my baby. My trust is in you, God I need you."

Don't allow the location of where you received the unfavorable or bad news to be the place you park out and die. Get up from where you are and produce. Don't sit there and die when your children are waiting for you and the people who are assigned to you are waiting for you. Don't just sit there and dry up because a disaster came in or a storm blew in and interrupted your schedule. Discover the reward in it. Discover what's on the other side of the storm. Why sit there and die when there is an abundant life waiting for you? Get up and begin again. Life happened! It happened! He or she walked out! You got fired! Your savings ran out! Someone close to you died! Your president didn't win! Whatever it is, get up from there and begin again. You know I am reminded of this story in the Bible where there were four leprous men. "They began to say to one another, why sit here and die? We already know that we are going to die here if we stay, BUT if we go out, there is no guarantee that we will die, we may live. Let's go in and see." 2 Kings 2:7

3 "And there were four leprous men at the entering in of the gate: and they said one to another, why sit here until we die? 4 "If we say, we will enter into the city, then the famine is in the city, and we shall die there: and if we sit still here, we die also. Now therefore come, and let us fall unto the host of the Syrians: if they

save us alive, we shall live; and if they kill us, we shall but die." 5 "And they rose up in the twilight, to go unto the camp of the Syrians: and when they were come to the uttermost part of the camp of Syria, behold, there was no man there." 6 "For the Lord had made the host of the Syrians to hear a noise of chariots, and a noise of horses, even the noise of a great host: and they said one to another, Lo, the king of Israel hath hired against us the kings of the Hittites, and the kings of the Egyptians, to come upon us." 7 "Wherefore they arose and fled in the twilight, and left their tents, and their horses, and their asses, even the camp as it was, and fled for their life." 8 "And when these lepers came to the uttermost part of the camp, they went into one tent, and did eat and drink, and carried thence silver, and gold, and raiment, and went and hid it; and came again, and entered into another tent, and carried thence also, and went and hid it."

Watch this, not only did God cause them to live but when the four leprous men got up at twilight at the same time, God caused the Syrians to hear a loud noise of chariots. The four leprous men's faith caused the Syrians to flee. Yes, the very ones they thought would kill them, end up leaving the camp. Not only did they leave the camp, but because they fled, the four men were able to eat, drink, and carry away silver, gold, and raiment. What if they would've stayed right there in fear and stuck in diagnoses of leprosy. What will happen if you stay where you are and never discover what's on the other side of your dark season? What may appear to be deadly could very well be your season of entering an abundant life. Don't sit there because prosperity, salvation, deliverance, your business, your books, your legacies await you.

Justace was calling for me, and I had to see her. When I heard her name and that she needed me, I got up. Justace is one part of my purpose. See your purpose should cause resurrected power to activate within you. Your purpose in life will cause you to get up and go beyond disastrous moments and seasons in your life.

Watch this, in Proverbs 19:21 it reads:

New International Version: "Many are the plans in a man's heart, but only God's purpose will prevail." It was God's purpose in me that caused me to prevail that day.

Many people get caught in excuses and bad news. Well, guess what? Yes, bad things happened to you, and yes it was painful, but why would you rob yourself of the next place in life? Life doesn't stop at bad news. Understand that this too shall pass and greater awaits you! I got up so others could get up. I got up so Justace could get up. I got up so I could write this book one day and tell somebody else I know what it's like to be down, but I also know what it's like to get up again. Was it fearful for me? Yes!!! But when I understood that God didn't give me the spirit of fear but that of power, love, and a sound mind, I had to release the negativity that was trying to hold me down. At all cost, we must release the excuses and move forward. Let me ask you a question. What happened to you that was so bad that you want to give up….. Get up and live the life God created you to live! What happened to you that was so bad that it is causing you to hate where you are but yet, you live there every day? What happened in your life that caused you to be angry with God? Anything that makes you mad enough should cause you to resolve the issue. Be angry but sin not. You should get angry enough to go to God. Talk to Him, pray to Him, and meditate on Him. I promise you that after you've finished, you will understand that it's not God's fault. God has a plan and purpose for you. When bad things happen to you, always remember Jeremiah 29: 11. It's one of my top five:

"For I know the thoughts that I think toward you saith the Lord, thoughts of peace and not of evil to give you an expected end."

God knows the thoughts, this means he already had a relationship with the thoughts He thinks towards us. When evil is coming toward you, understand that it is not God's thought. His thoughts are of peace and not of evil that leads to an expected end. Why would the loving, gracious, and merciful God we serve, cause harm to us? When bad things happen, people are so quick to blame God and question Him. This is the world in which we live. God is a loving God. He's a God of unity. He wants to produce life in us that we can create life within others. We are going to be the only God that some people will ever see. Stop being so angry with God. Understand evil manifestations come from the enemy and the demonic forces are trying to demolish your destiny. Stop questioning God and question yourself and see if you are in the faith. It may not feel good, but it's working for your good. I'm only able to talk about this because I been there. I remember thinking, "God I live holy. I am a single mother. I'm out here winning souls and preaching the gospel. God, why did you let this happen, aren't you powerful enough to stop it?" Yes, I thought about these things and several questions. I couldn't understand it for the life of me. Why me? Why my daughter.

First, I had to release the hurt, pain, and anger so I could hear God and know that He was with me. My focus had to shift to the fact that He was entirely on my side giving me the strength to stand and endure. According to:

Philippians 4:6 "For I am confident of this very thing, that He who began a good work in you will perfect it until the day of Christ Jesus."

Being convinced that He had already given me dominion to get past this storm. I got up from that chair that day with authority, knowing that my God shall supply all my needs according to His riches in glory! And that, this too shall pass.

Chapter Thirteen
The Long Walk

So here it was, I got up, and I'm walking to ICU, and it felt like the longest walk ever. I remember how long the hallway looked as I journeyed towards my baby.

Psalm 142: 3 "When my spirit was overwhelmed within me, then thou knewest my path."

But I had to get past it. I had to remind myself that this too shall pass. Just getting to the other side was on my mind. I remember the children of Israel crossing the Red Sea. God created a passage for them and created walls in the midst of a hopeless situation. When a deadly case presented itself, they didn't sit at the seashore and die. They got up and walked on dry ground. Not only were they able to go forward but the waters became a wall for them. God lead them the long way around. Because if they had taken the shortened passage, the Philistines would've probably made them afraid and they would've gone back to the Egyptians. There was a shorter way, but God led them through a more extended passage. God led them away and that caused their enemy's destruction. You see if the children of Israel hadn't gone by way of the Red Sea, the Egyptians would have never died. Also, if the Egyptians never died, they would have always pursued the children of Israel. But the way the Lord led them provided an opportunity for the enemies to no longer attack them. Let's look at it.

Exodus 14: 21 "And Moses stretched out his hand over the sea; the LORD caused the sea to go back by a strong east wind all that night, and made the sea dry land, and the waters were divided."

22 "And the children of Israel went into the midst of the sea upon the dry ground: and the waters were a wall unto them on their right hand, and on their left." 23 "And the Egyptians pursued and went in after them to the midst of the sea, even all Pharaoh's horses, his chariots, and his horsemen." 24 "And it came to pass, that in the morning watch the LORD looked unto the host of the Egyptians through the pillar of fire and of the cloud, and troubled the host of the Egyptians," 25 "And took off their chariot wheels, that they drave them heavily: so that the Egyptians said, Let us flee from the face of Israel; for the LORD fighteth for them against the Egyptians." 26 "And the LORD said unto Moses, Stretch out thine hand over the sea, that the waters may come again upon the Egyptians, upon their chariots, and upon their horsemen." "27 And Moses stretched forth his hand over the sea, and the sea returned to his strength when the morning appeared, and the Egyptians fled against it, and the LORD overthrew the Egyptians in the midst of the sea." 28 "And the waters returned and covered the chariots, and the horsemen, and all the host of Pharaoh that came into the sea after them; there remained not so much as one of them." 29 "But the children of Israel walked upon dry land in the midst of the sea, and the waters were a wall unto them on their right hand, and on their left." 30 "Thus the LORD saved Israel that day out of the hand of the Egyptians, and Israel saw the Egyptians dead upon the sea shore." 31 "And Israel saw that great work which the LORD did upon the Egyptians: and the people feared the LORD, and believed the LORD, and his servant Moses."

When I got to ICU, my daughter was up and looking for her dad and myself. Oh my, she grabbed my hand, and I called her name. Tears rolled down my face when I saw the tube going up her nose and the IVs in her arms and the bag hanging from the bed. Just yesterday, we were at Frankie's running around having a great time. Just two weeks ago, I was taking her to school and cooking dinner in the comfort of our home. Now we're in ICU with tubes and machines surrounded by us. I was trying to sneak a tear in because again, I didn't want her to see me crying. I was hiding behind my hair. I would slightly hold my head down because I felt like I was about to break into a million pieces. I was not supposed to see my baby like this; she should be home having a good time, fussing & fighting with her little sister, running up and down the stairs, telling me that Jordin just spilled nail polish on the carpet or telling me that Jordin wrote on walls. (I longed for these times again) I wanted it to be anything but cancer and ICU. Oh, how I longed for those days when I ran upstairs and said, "If you two don't stop, I'm going to take the iPad or change the WIFI password." I just wanted to go back to normal. I said to myself, "God I knew it was something, but God I didn't know it was this bad." So I'm behind my hair and crying trying to wipe my tears quickly with the one hand that Justace is not holding. Then I said, "Do you need Mommy to get you anything?" Her dad was right there trying to keep it all together as well. And lo and behold Justace said, "Can y'all rap? Yes, I want y'all to say a rap?" We looked at each other and just busted out laughing. Oh, I so needed that laugh. I said, "Huh?" She said, "Yes mommy and daddy, I want y'all to rap." It was like every tear of pain had turned into an ocean of laughter. I no longer felt the need to hide my tears; I just let them flow. I don't know what I said in the rap, but you betta believe mommy and daddy were rapping. How do you rap with someone you almost can't stand? Wow, how do you go from seeing each other a few times a year to all of a sudden every day, all day, in a small hospital room? All because you have a daughter with this person who is depending on you? Only with God, you can do it. Once I allowed God to help me get through each moment, it became better to process. But it was still hard for me. My entire life had changed. My daughter has cancer, and I am rapping with my ex-husband. What a combination that if someone would've told me, I wouldn't've believed them.

Some may wonder why she asked us to rap. Well, on our daily routines to school about three weeks before going to Duke, out the blue, I started rapping with Justace and Jordin. I was just making the morning trip to school fun and exciting. After all, it's the morning time, and we might as well have a great day. So I would make up something silly like, "My name is, my name is Candace, and I am the baddest, Justace is my baby even though she drives me crazy!" Cute little powerful fun moments that made our family time joyous and exciting. My girls and I find balance as much as possible because we go hard with school and ministry, so we have to have fun. Fun is a must in my household.

I tried my hardest not to be on the phone when going to school until they both dropped off in order to give them my full attention. I rapped, they rapped, and we'd go back and forth until they got to school. It was just one of those things we did. But this cute little fun moment became the most significant moment of my life in ICU. Yes, the rap was a major for the Joyner's! What if I had been too busy on the phone or in a bad mood that day, I choose to rap on the way to school just a few weeks prior? What if I was having a bad morning and didn't know how to honor my daughters with a fun morning before they got off to school? It's amazing the ideas God gives to parents to help reduce stress, but we become so busy and caught up in life that we can't have a moment to laugh. Laughter does the heart good; it's definitely medicine "A merry heart doeth good like a medicine: but a broken spirit drieth the bones (Psalm 17:22). So her dad and I went back and forth, rapping until we couldn't rap anymore. It was fun, and we needed it at that moment. Of course, the medication the doctors were giving her caused her to go in and out of sleep for the rest of the day. She slept, and we just looked at her. I moved the chair all the way up to the bed and just sat right there. Only one person can sleep in ICU, so her dad and I had to become a team again. Wow, how do you become a team with someone you haven't had a relationship with in years? Again, her dad lived in another city, and we didn't see him that much. How do you become a team with someone you divorced years ago? Now you're trapped in a small room together having to make decisions because it's no longer about you and how you feel, but what's best for the child and helping her get through a difficult time in her life. She may be reacting from medication but in a couple of days after the medicine wears off, what are you going to do?

That day, I had to make a real decision to forgive because I would look at him, remember all that I endured and went through. I didn't hate him, but I hated what happened to me. We made it through that night in ICU. Matter of fact, he kept saying, "Candace, it's going to be alright." "God is with us." I would doze off and have the worst nightmares. Fear tried to grip me again. I remember looking at my daughter and thinking, "God, how much time do I have left with her?" Looking at my ex-husband wondering, "Why do I have to see him so much?" I'm accustomed to seeing him two to three times a year. Now, he's here twenty-four-seven in a small hospital room. What do you say to a person like that? How do you make it when your world has flipped upside down and inside out? How do you stay holy when you feel like you're ready to tell somebody off and just really let them have it? What do you do when you want to release, but you have to stay Godly and respect your child who is now fighting for her life?" Oh, it got real.

I found out that it's easier to forgive someone who you don't see than to forgive someone you do see. I had to do it all over again, and this time I had to do it the right way. I had to if I was going to operate in full dominion and authority that God had given me. I realized I didn't have time to play nor harbor any negative feelings. I had to release and demonstrate the love of God. Yes, I preach about that same love. Now I had to live what I preached. All I knew, when I saw him, I felt some type of way, and I knew that it wasn't right. I understood that although I had told him time and time again that I forgive him, that there was another level of forgiveness I didn't honor. I couldn't acknowledge it fully because we never had intimate time to do so. It was always quick and usually at a birthday party surrounded by other people. And I now understood that it would be impossible to pray, and get past this challenging storm with the negativity and the past in front of me. I had to learn how to forgive. So there were times we talked, and there were times we didn't. We were both thrown into a situation unexpectedly. He had a girlfriend, and I was engaged to be married. But we had to deal with it and be parents. It wasn't easy, but we had to do it. With our daughter being sick, it was complicated to have a successful relationship and tend to her needs. I just couldn't anymore. When I invite someone into my world, I want to give them my best. I couldn't provide my best anymore. I wanted to yield my full attention to my daughter, and that's what I decided to do. This decision was not the easiest, but it was best for me at the time. My engagement began to dwindle until it was over.

Neither of us asked for Justace to have cancer, but it was there. Neither of us wanted to live in the hospital for a week at a time, but we had too. Our lives changed in an instant. I remember not wanting anybody to find out about Justace. For some odd reason, I became ashamed. I just said I couldn't let anyone know about this. I don't know why, but I did. By that time, my family had intercessors praying for us. Thank you, God, because I remember pastors sending text messages. One Pastor told me, "God said, "It's done." I will never forget another text message; it read, "You have power in your hands. Utilize what you have." I remember after I woke up from that last nightmare, I got up, and I began to walk up and down in the room, praying, I lay hands on my daughter again. This exchange took place within hours after finding out the diagnosis. I got up, and I began to speak to it. I started to tell cancer to go and be far from us. I felt like I had my strength back because beforehand, I was lying there wondering how long do I have with my child. All of a sudden, I'm declaring she shall live and not die and declare the works of the Lord. Why? All because I received a text message that activated life. One of the best things you can ever do in the midst of a storm is to pray your way through. Prayer takes your focus off the problem and opens a communication tunnel with God. Not only in prayer are you talking, but you get quiet so that God can speak to you as well. Hear the profitable things God wants to deliver to you. Also, after you pray believe you receive. Take a moment to believe in God. Believe and see yourself having Godly results.

Scriptures on prayer:

Jonah 2:7 "When my soul fainted within me I remembered the LORD: and my prayer came in unto thee, into thine holy temple."

James 5:15 "And the prayer of faith shall save the sick, and the Lord shall raise him up; and if he has committed sins, they shall be forgiven him."

Colossians 4:2 "Continue in prayer, and watch in the same with thanksgiving;"

The next day was Day 7, and we moved back to the pediatric floor. We decided to get through this storm with the help of God. This storm began a spiritual movement in my life that some people did, and some did not understand. I had to make a decision that I knew would be best for my daughter and me at the time. I had to walk away from people, places, and things for my daughter to have courage. Besides, she needed my full attention. My life changed for the better after Day 6 of hearing the diagnosis of cancer that had already progressed to stage 4. It changed for the better because I was able to know God on a higher dimension than I knew Him before.

People talked about the decisions I made as it related to my daughter's recovery. I couldn't let that stop me. It wasn't so much the people in the world, as it was people in the church that tried to destroy my name or perhaps underestimate my position. All I knew was I was a holy woman, and if anyone wanted to imagine me in sin or error during the most challenging time of my life, they had to think again. I remember her dad coming to stay with us because we decided for our daughter to have the best care from both her parents. He had to leave Charlotte for a season to be by his daughter's side. That was extremely hard for me, but again, it wasn't about me, it was about Justace and that big bright smile she would have on her face when her parents became a team. Oh my, she kept us in check plenty of days. We became a significant aspect of her healing and deliverance. So we did what we needed to do to get the results we needed to get.

What results are you blocking from manifesting in your life? Are you willing to get uncomfortable? How bad do you want your miracle? I remember having to change my home attire because I had to be presentable around her dad. I didn't want to entice him. Our business was to get a miracle from God, and not allow the enemy to persuade us otherwise. Always stay focused on the process. I have always enjoyed my prayer area in my living room, but this particular season, I had to pray upstairs. I had opened up my living room for him to stay during chemotherapy. Honestly, my daughter's attitude was more positive with him around. He had a way to make her laugh and encourage her. I had to move Candace out the way, so Justace was restored. I wanted to share this because if I appear like everything I have ever done was easy; I wouldn't be truthful. I want this book to help someone who is dealing with similar challenges. Sometimes, when our friends and loved ones get sick, we are forced to see people we haven't seen in years. Sometimes, we are forced to interact with people we don't necessarily want to be around. It's not always easy, but it shows you how mature you are. It also demonstrates that you no longer give that situation power over you, you have power over it. In what area was I gaining power? I gained power over a spirit of, "Bump you or forget you, I've been doing it all by myself for five years, go back where you come from." Also, the bitterness that was resting within me showed its face. Candace had to come face to face with some things. But Candace got free. Some days, I pondered on the fact that Justace was the one diagnosed, but I was the one set free. I try to examine situations I find myself in and find out why I am involved and what part am I playing in this?

Finally, I conducted a self-examination, and I decided, don't let anything separate you from the love of God. No matter what, always show God's love. We can do all these things in life, but if we don't have love, we are nothing. This too shall pass if you so desire. How bad do you want it to pass? I didn't ask for bitterness, but I allowed what happened to me in my early twenties to mid-twenties to cause bitterness to form. I didn't know the capacity of it until my daughter's diagnosis. My God, could it be the storm that you are in causing you to see who you really are? Don't miss the reward of the storm. Find out who are you and obtain the reward. Get delivered in the storm. Find your freedom in the storm. As I write this book, I am so free!

Right now, I have a medical bill sitting on my counter for about $31,000.00. The very first bill I received in the mail was over $19,000.00. Because of the chemotherapy treatments and hospital admittance a week at a time, the medical bills went through the roof. I still believe God that all Justace's bills will be paid in full. A day after hearing about the diagnoses, a medical social worker was assigned to us. She suggested I start a GoFundMe page being that I was a full-time student, not working a 9-5 job. I also had a close friend demand I start one. They were so supportive and would assist me in any way I needed. I would often say, "No it's okay." It reminded me of my best friend who I watched endure the biggest storm of her life. She lost her husband. I watched her hurt and live through that catastrophic storm which taught me how to walk with strength. I would always say, "I don't know how you are doing this, this has to be God."

God was with her every step of the way. So God encircled me with people who could relate and uplift me. They suggested the GoFundMe. I was reluctant, but after a few weeks, I finally agreed to do it. So after contemplating on it, I released the GoFundMe page. I didn't want to do it because I didn't want people to know what was going on in my family. The amazing thing about the GoFundMe account is, it triggered so many people to pray for us. People we didn't know heard about Justace's story and immediately blessed us not only financially, but many prayed and sent encouraging words and gifts to her. We appreciated everything that everyone has done for us.

One day, I learned some people printed off my GoFundMe letter and critiqued what I wrote. They weren't in agreement with what I wrote. Selah. Here it is, I am a single mother with a daughter fighting for her life, asking those who would help us financially and through prayers, to please do so. I decided to discuss this portion of the GoFundMe because it is a needed part of this book. I want to help people understand that everybody you think is with you during your storm isn't always with you. Everybody that is on the outside looking in can't give you their advice. People who appeared to be with me argued with me about what they thought I should have said. Selah. The beautiful thing about any GoFundMe page is the fact that no one is obligated to participate. I didn't call anyone in particular to donate, the letter just asked for help. The beauty of asking a question is the right to say YES or NO! Why would someone want to argue with a mother during a challenging time such as this over what she said and didn't say? Selah. My response to these people was, if anyone felt like it was wrong, why could the person or group of people not just pick up the phone and call me or visit me to share their wisdom. Their response to me when I made contact was, "You don't even know the caliber of the people who were discussing you." I was hurt. I'm thinking to myself, "The caliber of the people," truly they can't be sent by God." But I was agitated. I believe that when a person sees someone in a hurting position, they should only help them or be quiet. I am not the perfect mother, but I do believe I have provided the best life I could have possibly give my two daughters. Especially as a single parent. It was hurtful that someone would argue with me about a GoFundMe page when I had "bigger fish to fry." My daughter was fighting for her life. Once again, I had to release them and the drama. I went to that person because it made me feel a certain way. Again, I didn't want to harbor anything in my heart. I was offended, so I dealt with it. Just like if they were offended, they should've come to me instead of eating me for breakfast, lunch, and dinner. I want the readers to know, just because you are in a storm doesn't mean no other hurt will knock on your door. It's bad enough when you are already in a storm, then, here come other unique cases you have to face. Understand that people will always be people. Everyone is entitled to their own opinion. But the word of God says it this way: "let God be true, but every man a liar. If you don't have anything profitable to say don't say it at all."

Psalm 57:2 "I call upon the God Most High; to the God who completes what he began in me. 3 He will send help from heaven to deliver me from those who harass and despise me."

Never allow people to judge you, let God be the judge of your situation. The next few months ahead of us were very peculiar, but we managed to make it. First and foremost, we only made it because of God. I am also thankful to the powerful intercessors who prayed with us during this time.

If I began discussing everything that happened next, this book would take several months to complete. I wanted to discuss the first seven days as well as when I first became pregnant with Justace. This portion of our lives was pivotal. I wanted to share a portion of my story, the way I was inspired. I want people to stay loyal to God even in the midst of the storms of life. This requires faith, dedication, and commitment. We should let nothing penetrate our faith. Storms come and sometimes are raging, but at the end of the day, "THIS TOO SHALL PASS."

Zechariah 10:11

"And he shall pass through the sea with affliction, and shall smite the waves in the sea, and all the deeps of the river shall dry up...."

I have gone through church hurt and church disappointment. I had received countless calls from other pastors wanting me to assist them in pastoring when they got word I left my previous church, but God did not lead me that way. I understood my time hadn't come yet to pastor God's people. I was instructed by God to go and be healed, strengthen, and fed spiritually. When God wants to restore you, He will give you His best. Some foolishly stated I went through that storm with my daughter because I left a church that God instructed me to leave. Not so! I respectfully submitted a letter to that ministry, and I moved forward in my life. No one is bound to stay at a church. Although it was hard to walk away from a ministry that I grew up in, my time had come to an end. I had to be obedient, and I charge anyone to do the same. I also charge Pastors to be mindful of the sheep and the words they speak unto them without getting in their flesh. The word of God states: Jeremiah 3:15 "And I will give you pastors according to mine heart, which shall feed you with knowledge and understanding."

I will say this, I believe witchcraft played a significant role in what happened with my child. I know it was an act sent from hell and all demonic forces. But I'm so glad I serve a God who is well able to see me through any demonic storm or activity.

Job 2:2 "And the LORD said unto Satan, From whence comest thou? And Satan answered the LORD, and said, From going to and fro in the earth, and from walking up and down in it." 1 Peter 5:8 "Be sober, be vigilant; because your adversary the devil, as a roaring lion, walketh about, seeking whom he may devour:"

2 Corinthians 2:11 "Lest Satan should get an advantage of us: for we are not ignorant of his devices."

You Can and Will overcome the enemy!

And Jesus answered and said unto him, "Get thee behind me, Satan: for it is written, Thou shalt worship the Lord thy God, and him only shalt thou serve."

I can end this book by saying my daughter and our family found out on June 30, 2016, that she was free from cancer. Because cancer is an infirmity, one should be delivered from it. This infirmity passed away from us, and God healed her body from all manner of sickness and disease. There was much prayer given during this time and seven months later, much prayer is still going forth on our behalf.

2 Thessalonians 2:11 "Wherefore also we pray always for you, that our God would count you worthy of this calling, and fulfill all the good pleasure of his goodness, and the work of faith with power:"

Chapter Fourteen
Scriptures To Empower You To Trust God

I found these scriptures to be very helpful and encouraging during my storm. Prayerfully, these scriptures can assist you. The Word helps us because when life is hard, we can continue in our faith that this too shall pass. Reading the word signifies that there is hope for me and this situation. I choose to trust God and not what I'm experiencing at the moment. Try reading the Word. Remember God has to watch over his word and bring it to pass.

Colossians 1:9 "For this cause we also, since the day we heard it, do not cease to pray for you, and to desire that ye might be filled with the knowledge of his will in all wisdom and spiritual understanding;"

Psalm 50:15 "And call upon me in the day of trouble: I will deliver thee, and thou shalt glorify me."

Romans 8:18 "For I reckon that the sufferings of this present time are not worthy to be compared with the glory which shall be revealed in us."

2 Corinthians 4:17 "For our light affliction, which is but for a moment, worketh for us a far more exceeding and eternal weight of glory;"

2 Timothy 2:10 "Therefore I endure all things for the elect's sakes, that they may also obtain the salvation which is in Christ Jesus with eternal glory."

2 Corinthians 1: 3 "Blessed be God, even the Father of our Lord Jesus Christ, the Father of mercies, and the God of all comfort;" 4 "Who comforteth us in all our tribulation, that we may be able to comfort them which are in any trouble, by the comfort wherewith we ourselves are comforted of God." 5 "For as the sufferings of Christ abound in us, so our consolation also aboundeth by Christ." 6 "And whether we be afflicted, it is for your consolation and salvation, which is effectual in the enduring of the same sufferings which we also suffer: or whether we be comforted, it is for your consolation and salvation." 7 "And our hope of you is stedfast, knowing, that as ye are partakers of the sufferings, so shall ye be also of the consolation."

This book was written to inform you God loves you so much. He will perform His word and bring it to pass for your situation to pass. Remember your life can't stay in turmoil forever. You cannot continue to hurt forever, and you cannot continue to go through pain forever, you cannot live with unforgiveness forever, you just cannot. Your life is worth so much more than the negatively that lingers around you. Get up and make a difference in your life today. Keep the mindset that THIS TOO SHALL PASS!

This Too Shall Pass Prayer:

Heavenly Father, I come humbly before you as I know how. We ask you to forgive us our sins and to create in us a clean heart and renew the right spirit within us. Take not your Holy Spirit away from me. Today, I decree and declare that no weapon formed against me shall prosper. I put on the whole armor of God and quench every fiery dart of the enemy. I choose to operate in total dominion and authority that God has already given me. I am the righteousness of God in Christ Jesus. I am covered by the blood of Jesus and by His stripes, I am healed. Because I understand that this too shall pass in my life, I pray that my faith fails me not. God, I believe you but help my unbelief. Strengthen me for the journey and the expected end you promised unto me. I decree and declare that I will get to the other side of this storm. I will not die in this storm, but I will live and declare the works of the Lord. I decree and declare that I will prosper and bring glory to God in all I pursue. Father, I pray for the mindset to trust you at all times even when it doesn't look good. I decree what I see is only temporal and that the best is yet ahead of me. Father allow my assigned angels to work for me in every capacity needed. I thank you that any form of sickness, disease, infirmity, and destruction is far from me, my children, my family, and loved ones. We're covered and wrapped in your loving arms. Keep us at all times and let nothing come upon us unaware. Allow my eyes to stay toward you and my ears attentive to what you are saying. I want to experience the fullness of you and the abundant life that you have orchestrated for my life. I command every foul spirit, demonic spirit, and any other spirit that is not inspired by God to flee from me, my children, and my family. I decree we win and victory is ours! Father, I release these prayers toward you, believing that it's already done and that this storm that I am in will pass! I decree and declare this too shall pass in Jesus name, Amen!

Homework:

What is in your life that you would like to see pass?

1.

2.

3.

4.

What is your next step in making this happen?

_____

What are your fears? Is anything stopping you?

_____

What victories do you see beyond this point? You must see it and believe it!

1.

2.

3.

4.

5.

NOW DO IT EVEN IF YOU DO IT AFRAID! IT IS TIME TO LIVE BEYOND THIS MOMENT!

What is your vision because there is a greater you? Begin here but finish writing it out later. Because after this passes by, you need to live out HIS MATERPLAN FOR YOUR LIFE!

My vision:

This Too Shall Pass
(journal your thoughts)

This Too Shall Pass
(journal your thoughts)

This Too Shall Pass
(journal your thoughts)

I believe you are the next author (fill in below):

The name of my book is:

_____

This is my signature for my book signing:

_____

The name of my business is:

_____

        You are off to a great start, now do something!

ABOUT THE AUTHOR

Candace is a very dedicated mother. She is a Prophet of God and stands in the role of Pastor of Empowerment Kingdom Center. She has committed her life as a 21st-century Intercessor. She has gained an international voice in many capacities and enjoy the opportunity to demonstrate the real life of a servant of God. Candace enjoys serving and helping people. After finding a passion for serving people not only in ministry, she also embraced helping and empowering people in the secular realm as well. Candace is a Licensed Clinical Social Worker Associate. She enjoys counseling and assisting people in bringing them hope, introducing them to resilience and living an empowered life. She is a life-learner and she's pursuing her educational goals as a second-time master student to help facilitate her dreams, goals, and vision. She is a woman with a mandate and doesn't mind breaking impossible barriers to live out supernatural manifestations. She now understands whatever is in her way, that this too shall pass and greater shall be the reward.

Follow Candace on

YouTube, Facebook, Instagram, Twitter, and any social media outlet.

Email contact: iwillpursue@gmail.com

Candace Joyner, MSW, LCSWA, LCASA, BSW

For all your book publishing needs please contact us! Let's make your book dream a reality. Your words hold value, and your readers are waiting!

Join our Author's Empowerment Program and get started today.

CONTACT US TODAY

www.candacejoyner.com

Candacejoyner2020@gmail.com

P.O. BOX 310
Lumberton NC 28358

(910) 416-9988

www.ingramcontent.com/pod-product-compliance
Lightning Source LLC
Chambersburg PA
CBHW031435150426
43191CB00006B/533